TED DEKKER
WITH BILL VANDERBUSH

THE
FORGOTTEN
WAY

STUDY GUIDE

D1362218

GETTING STARTED

Do you remember the parable of Jesus in which a master throws a banquet and invites many to come feast with him? The problem is, everyone seems to have an excuse. One has bought a cow and cannot come. Another has married a wife and is preoccupied. Still another must tend to his fields.

In the story, the master rises up and sends his servants to find any who will come—lame, blind, poor, vagabond, whoever will. And so they come, the outcasts of society, to feast at his table.

We tend to think this story deals only with the afterlife, but we've missed His point. The Father's feast awaits us each day. Our problem is that we are often too busy. The world and all of its concerns distract us from answering that invitation each day, all day. His call to us is clear: deny the world daily, sit at His table, taste and see that He is good.

There is no time more important than the half hour you give to this journey each day, so do not grow too weary or too busy to come to the table. Seek you first the kingdom and all that other stuff will be added to you. If you don't, all that other stuff will eventually suffocate you.

If you are reading this, you've been called. So then, be encouraged and make haste. Many are called, but few answer. You are clearly among the few.

THIS STUDY GUIDE IN A NUTSHELL

This Study Guide is divided into three themed sections: The Truth, The Way, and The Life. Within those themes are five Declarations that summarize the five principles of *The Forgotten Way*. Each of the 21 lessons begin with a brief reflection on the corresponding study from *The Forgotten Way Meditations*. Included with each lesson are a series of Scriptures with insight that are coordinated with the numbers from each of the 21 lessons in *The Forgotten Way Meditations*. Finally, there are a series of questions for personal study and group discussion. If you are doing this study alone, rather than writing in the lines provided, you might want to write in a separate journal as the questions will often provoke a longer answer than the lines provided can contain.

If you are doing this study in a group, these questions are designed to invite transparency and provoke dynamic discussion. Pay close attention to moments when you hear a word or have a thought that is refreshing and life-giving to your spirit. Those are the ones you will want to write down.

At the end of some of the questions you will see an activation. This is designed to put some action to what you've learned. It's not enough to know a concept in your mind alone. Every revelation you receive from God is an invitation to an encounter and it's often in the action that we gain understanding and wisdom that mere thought could never produce.

SOME THOUGHTS BEFORE YOU BEGIN

As we dive into the scriptures from the meditations, it's important that you understand a few things about how spiritual insights come to people. We have the freedom to hate, the challenge to love, and enough verses in the Bible to support both vengeance and grace. Using the Bible, you can support doctrines of heaven, hell, healing, salvation, sickness, tribulation, dispensation, torment, pleasure, grief, joy, wrath, and grace, both universal and conditional.

Have you ever wondered how one book that's meant to reveal God has itself been such a launching pad for conflict and division? Likely because as it reveals Him, it also reveals the conflict within each of us. The Bible reads you far more than you read it. The Word reveals you to yourself, and in doing so, it exposes your perspective of your Father.

For many years, the question has persisted, "Who am I in Christ?" The greater question, however, might be, "Who is Christ, in me?" Because until you get a revelation of who He is, everything you think about who you are is merely a guess.

When you get a revelation that the One from whom all faith originates believes in you, then that belief holds you. It is in that place that you are at rest and secure. Pure doctrine and authentic belief is simply saying yes to what God believes about you. God believes some amazing things about you, and what God believes about you is what reveals who you truly are.

Being "in Him" is the Divine reality that empowers the awakening of your true identity.

Here's why this matters. What you believe becomes the reality that you experience. We are created in the likeness of our creator to manifest that which we believe to be true. This is the power of faith. What we believe, we behold, and what we behold becomes our experience. If you believe you are separated from your Father as a Christian, you will interpret the Bible through that lens of a broken or fragile relationship.

However, if you accept that you are in Him and that there is no distance, no separation, between you and your Father right now, and that you can't stop the endless flood of His mercy for you, then the Bible stops being a confusing book of conflicting commandments and becomes a beautiful revelation of Love Himself. Being in Him doesn't make you God, just as being in you doesn't make Him you. However, you are one, together. This is a great mystery, but as with many of God's wonders, your heart can know and delight in what your mind may not yet fully understand.

All of Scripture, all relationship, all of life, all identity, all of time, every mystery is illuminated in the light of this basic revelation. **You are one with God in Christ by the power of the Spirit.** Your Father, God (who is Love, Peace, Joy, Father, Son, Holy Spirit) is one within you right now by His desire and design. I have a great passion for all people to walk in the light rather than in darkness, particularly those Christians who live in blindness to their own identity, already complete in Christ.

In this regard, Paul offers both great encouragement and a warning when he writes: *See to it that no one takes you captive through philosophy and empty deception, according to the tradition of men, according to the elementary principles of the world, rather than according to Christ. For in Him all the fullness of Deity dwells in bodily form,* **and in Him you have been made complete,** *and He is the head over all rule and authority.* (*Colossians 2:8-10*)

So then, we who believe Jesus's declaration that we are in Him and He is in us, even as He is in the Father, have great cause to rejoice. God is good, and now we too, are good, at our very core, because in Him there is no darkness and now He is in us and we are in Him. Discovering this reality is the journey of your life and it's wrapped up in the following declarations.

THE TRUTH

1) God is infinitely good, far more loving and gentle and kind to His children than any earthly mother or father imaginable. **God is infinitely complete**; nothing can threaten or disturb Him. Nothing can be taken away from Him, making Him less than complete, nor added to Him who is already complete.

2) You are remade in the likeness and glory of your Father, finite yet already complete in union with Yeshua—you in Him and He in you, risen with Him and seated in heavenly places. Nothing can separate you from His love.

THE WAY

3) Your journey now is to see who you truly are, for you are the light of the world, the son or the daughter of your Father, a new creature flowing with more beauty and power than you dared imagine possible.

4) You will only *see* who you are and thus *be* who you are as you surrender your attachment to all other identities, which are like gods of a lesser power that block your vision of your true identity and keep you in darkness.

THE LIFE

5) Love, joy, and peace are the manifestation of your true identity and the Father's realm, on earth as in heaven through the power of the Holy Spirit.

I

THE TRUTH

Yeshua made it plain: *I am the Way, the Truth and the Life.*

In the first section we will enter seven meditations on the simplest *Truth* about, first, who the *Father* is (meditations 1-3) and, second, who *you* are, as the son or the daughter of the Father through Yeshua (meditations 4-7).

These constitute the first and second declarations of The Forgotten Way.

THE FIRST DECLARATION

God is infinitely good, *far more loving and gentle and kind to His children than any earthly mother or father imaginable.* **God is infinitely complete**; *nothing can threaten or disturb Him. Nothing can be taken away from Him, making Him less than complete, nor added to Him who is already complete.*

THE SECOND DECLARATION

You are remade in the likeness and glory of your Father, *finite yet already complete in union with Yeshua—you in Him and He in you, risen with Him and seated in heavenly places. Nothing can separate you from His love.*

ONE

LOOK HOW MAGNIFICENT YOUR FATHER

"Where did you come from? What is your origin? But more, who is your Father? You must know this to begin to experience your own identity on this earth."

WHO IS YOUR FATHER?

Our entire lives in every respect are deeply influenced by our view of our origin, our source, where we came from, who God is. Many people live fiercely independent and seem to have made God in their own image, which is only a form of idolatry. We tend to think God thinks the way we do, and feels threatened like we do; that He can somehow experience fear of loss which is at the core of all negative emotions.

But this is not God. God is infinitely complete and without weakness of vulnerability in any aspect, and therefore He cannot possibly feel threatened or fear loss. Jesus, being both fully God and fully human, experienced what we experience in every way, which is part of the beauty of His incarnation.

But His Father and your own, in whose likeness you are created, is both closer than your own breath, and transcendent, perfectly and uncompromisingly complete. He always has been, long before He created this universe. And He will be forever.

Your refuge is in Him. The story the teacher tells of the lion and the hyena simply conveys this beautiful mystery.

Everyone who has spent any time alive can attest to this fact. Life seems out of control. Just when you think you've made enough money to be at peace, an unexpected expense arises. Just when you believe you've worked out enough to be considered physically fit, you suffer a setback you didn't expect and find yourself in pain. Just when you feel the warmth of a secure relationship, a challenge of betrayal threatens your sense of belonging.

Here's the truth: your circumstances *are* out of your control, ending inevitably in your physical death no matter how hard you might try to change it.

When you begin to see who your Father really is, you will then begin to trust Him. And as you trust Him, you will surrender the control you don't have to the One who alone is trustworthy to control.

Yielding the reigns of your life is the beginning of faith in God.

REFLECT ON THESE QUESTIONS

1. If your Father is infinitely complete in and of Himself, does He ever have new thoughts that surprise Him like they would a human mind? If He already has infinite knowledge of all things, present and future beyond time, how could He discover a new thought?

_____

_____

2. If you think your Father can be compromised and is therefore not infinitely complete and powerful, then write one sentence that characterizes the God you believe in.

_____

_____

3. If God always knew you before the foundations of this world, when did your existence begin? When did your experience in flesh begin?

_____

_____

4. Even before He created this universe, God already knew everything you would ever do. If you believe it's possible, explain how He could be disappointed by having an outcome different than what He foreknew.

_____

_____

5. How would you feel if your Father told you that He's so taken by you that, unlike an earthly father, He's never been disappointed in you? Would it repel you or draw you to Him?

_____

_____

ACTIVATION

Think of someone (pay attention to the first person that comes to your mind) who needs to know they are loved by their Father. Take a moment today to communicate with them in person or with a phone call. But before you do, ask the Father what His heart is for them and from a pure heart say to them, "Your Father's love for you is infinite. He's so proud of you and isn't disappointed in you." Does this seem like a hard thing to say? Can you say it to yourself? When you awaken to the Father's love for you, giving it away will become natural.

SCRIPTURES AND REFLECTIONS FROM THE MEDITATION

1. *Genesis 1:26 Then God said, "Let us make man in Our image, after Our likeness."*
Man was made to live in an intimate communion with God, glorified with the very image and identity of God, animated by His very breath, the empowering holiness of His Spirit. You were made to live in God, and He in you. He is our life, our breath, our love, our joy, our peace. It is God Himself who defines who you are. The work of Jesus is to restore us to this identity.

2. *Jeremiah 1:5 Before I formed you in the womb I knew you. Ephesians 1:3-4 Blessed be the God and Father of our Lord Jesus Christ,*

who has blessed us with every spiritual blessing in the heavenly places in Christ, just as He chose us in Him **before the foundation of the world***, that we would be holy and blameless before Him.*

Before God even said, "Let there be light," we existed in the mind of God. This is a profound and wonderful mystery, because it means that you existed as the pure and creative knowledge of God even before the formation and fall of the cosmos.

3. *Ephesians 1:5-7 In love He predestined us to adoption as sons through Jesus Christ to Himself, according to the kind intention of His will, to the praise of the glory of His grace, which He freely bestowed on us in the Beloved.*

4. *John 1:1-5 In the beginning was the Word, and the Word was with God, and the Word was God. He was in the beginning with God. All things came into being through Him, and apart from Him nothing came into being that has come into being. In Him was life, and the life was the Light of men. The Light shines in the darkness, and the darkness did not comprehend it.*

5. *Acts 17:28 In Him we live and move and exist, as even some of your own poets have said, "For we also are His children."*

Your origin and identity are in Him. To be able to see yourself in Him is a challenge if you have grown up to believe that you and God are separated. Are you separated from Christ? Our brother, Paul, would say emphatically "no." Jesus Himself expressed this in **John 14:20**: *In that day you will know that I am in My Father and you in Me and I in you.*

6. *1 John 3:1-2 See how great a love the Father has bestowed on us, that we would be called children of God; and such we are. For this reason the world does not know us, because it did not know Him. Beloved, now we are children of God, and it has not appeared as yet what we will be. We know that when He appears, we will be like Him, because we will see Him just as He is.*

Is there any more secure meditation than this reality that God would grant us an identity as His children? It wasn't the result of your ability to impress Him. It's a gift of great love.

TWO

THERE IS NO FEAR IN LOVE

*"Before you can know who you are,
you must know your Father."*

THERE'S KNOWING AND THEN THERE'S *KNOWING!*

Picture a father filled with delight at his two-year-old daughter. She can't spell the word "love" let alone explain it. But that doesn't stop this father from sweeping her up in his arms, swinging her around, and dancing with her. It also doesn't stop her from laughing loudly and smiling uncontrollably saying, "Daddy!" What kind of father would he be if he withheld his love from her because she wasn't mature enough or educated enough to understand the concept?

What hinders your delight in experiencing things of the Spirit? Are you holding back because you don't believe you understand enough about God or the Bible? Perhaps you were convinced by someone that you weren't spiritually mature. Just because you don't fully grasp the concept of the love, grace, or goodness of your Father, doesn't mean that you can't delight in experiencing it.

Many Christians secretly hold on to fear because of their view of God, often without even realizing it. In their mind, God's punishment is what they were saved from, but this leaves them with a fear of the Father who would punish them if Jesus had not rescued them from God's punishment. John is clear, there is no fear in love because fear has to do with punishment and God's love isn't about punishment.

The fear of the Lord is a beautiful thing, but not if you incorrectly define fear as anything but awe. Hosea 3:5 speaks of a people who come trembling to the Lord and His goodness. Without a revelation of the goodness of God, your fear of your Father will keep you from experiencing His presence even though nothing can separate you from His love.

It is your "yes" that allows you to become aware of His goodness. Close your eyes, tip your head back, breathe in, and drink deeply of this beautiful truth. You are loved, accepted, and cherished by your Father.

REFLECT ON THESE QUESTIONS

1. How is your earthly father like or unlike your heavenly Father?

_____

_____

2. Describe a time in your life when you knew your Father was good and loved you.

_____

_____

3. What are some practical moments where you have tasted and seen that the Father is good?

_____

_____

4. If God were to punish you, how would He do it and why?

_____

_____

ACTIVATION

When you know God loves and accepts you, seeing Him isn't a problem anymore. Close your eyes and simply imagine Jesus standing in front of you. Please understand that this is not a new age visualization exercise, but simply a purposeful focus of your childlike imagination that will reveal something important about *you*. Take a few moments to focus on

Him. Linger for a minute, considering how you are picturing Him and then open your eyes.

If you're in a group, discuss how you pictured Him. Was He smiling, joyful, laughing, happy? Frowning, angry, or looking away? Did He speak anything as you were looking at Him? You might be surprised. This will give you an indication of how you or members of the group perceive how Jesus sees them. Go ahead, try again.

SCRIPTURES AND REFLECTIONS FROM THE MEDITATION

1. *John 17:3 This is eternal life, that they may know You, the only true God, and Jesus Christ whom You have sent.*

2. *Matthew 18:3 Truly I say to you, unless you are converted and become like children, you will not enter the kingdom of heaven. Matthew 11:25 Jesus said, "I praise You, Father, Lord of heaven and earth, that You have hidden these things from the wise and intelligent and have revealed them to infants."*

3. *Psalm 34:8 O taste and see that the Lord is good; How blessed is the man who takes refuge in Him!*

When you truly experience (know) your Father, you will see that He is very good. There is a great difference between information and revelation.

4. *1 John 4:18 There is no fear in love; but perfect love casts out fear, because fear involves punishment, and the one who fears is not perfected in love.*

Love and fear are two of the most powerful motivators of human behavior. I've heard of people who are scared *of* falling in love, but once the love comes, the fear goes. I have never heard of anyone who was scared *into* falling in love. Yet I have spoken with many people whose relationship with God was motivated by a fear of hell rather than a love of God. And for many, that fear is what motivates them to this day.

How is it for you? If you are like many others who first responded to God out of fear, you may find that over time, cold, mechanical distance seems to separate you from God. I pray every sense of unhealthy fear is replaced with an awe-inspired love for your Father in whom there is no fear, because there is no fear in love.

5. *Psalm 111:10* ESV *The fear of the Lord is the beginning of wisdom; all those who practice it have a good understanding.*

There are a few Hebrew terms for *fear*. One is *Pachad*, which is "fear whose objects are imagined." We all have the defensive power to anticipate what may be and can become afraid of something that doesn't even exist. A completely opposite term, the word used in Psalm 111:10, is *Yirah,* which is "the fear that overwhelms us when we suddenly find ourselves in the presence of (or in possession of) considerably more power (wealth, authority, or influence) than we are used to."

6. *Psalm 103:10-13 He has not dealt with us according to our sins, Nor rewarded us according to our iniquities. For as high as the heavens are above the earth, So great is His lovingkindness toward those who fear Him. As far as the east is from the west, So far has He removed our transgressions from us. Just as a father has compassion on his children, So the Lord has compassion on those who fear Him.*

How far is the east from the west? This is not a description of distance, but a metaphor that transcends any measurable space. To put it simply, your transgressions no longer exist. Did you notice that this is in the Old Testament? David caught sight of the mercy of God in the middle of one of the most dysfunctional family dynamics in history. Even prior to Jesus's arrival in the flesh, David sees the heart of the Father. The only thing God intends to separate us from is our sin. The love of your Father is so great that He desires to remove every barrier to your union with Him.

7. *John 14:9 Jesus said to him, "Have I been so long with you, and yet you have not come to know Me, Philip? He who has seen Me has seen the Father." John 10:30 I and the Father are one. John 5:18 For this cause therefore the Jews were seeking all the more to kill Him, because He not only was breaking the Sabbath, but also was calling God His own Father, making Himself equal with God. Colossians 2:9 For in Him all the fullness of Deity dwells in bodily form. 2 Corinthians 5:19 God was in Christ*

reconciling the world to Himself, not counting their trespasses against them, and He has committed to us the word of reconciliation.

This is such a beautiful mystery. In the same way that Jesus was one with the Father, in Him you are rejoined with the Father.

8. *Matthew 23:9 Do not call anyone on earth your father; for One is your Father, He who is in heaven. 1 Corinthians 8:6 ESV Yet for us there is one God, the Father, from whom are all things and for whom we exist, and one Lord, Jesus Christ, through whom are all things and through whom we exist. Ephesians 4:6 ESV One God and Father of all, who is over all and through all and in all. Romans 8:15 For you have not received a spirit of slavery leading to fear again, but you have received a spirit of adoption as sons by which we cry out, "Abba! Father!"*

No matter how your father in this world has been, ultimately in God we have a very good Father.

9. *Romans 8:38-39 For I am convinced that neither death, nor life, nor angels, nor principalities, **nor things present, nor things to come**, nor powers, nor height, nor depth, nor any other created thing, will be able to separate us from the love of God, which is in Christ Jesus our Lord.*

Did you notice what's missing here? The one thing not included in this list is the past, and that's because your past isn't even relevant. Your Father loves you so deeply that He refuses to allow your past, your failures, your sins, your offenses, to dictate to Him whether or not He can love you. There is nothing in the present and nothing in the future that can threaten your Father's love for you. Let the eternal reality of your Father's love erase any foreboding anticipation of the unknown. This reality is your rest. You are loved by your Father right now, where you are, as you are.

THREE

THE STORY OF YOUR FATHER

"Remember your beautiful Father who holds your robe and your ring and your seat at his table even now, eagerly awaiting for you to celebrate who you truly are."

A TALE OF TWO SONS

No doubt you're familiar with the parable that we call *The Prodigal Son.* Jesus didn't give the story that name. We did. But a closer look at the parable reveals that perhaps we were wrong in our assessment. First of all, there are two prodigals, both who removed themselves from the Father's table. Furthermore, neither is the main character.

The story would better be called, *The Father's Heart.* One son asks for his inheritance, which you would only receive when the father dies. So this son basically says to his father, "I wish you were dead." That's shocking in any culture, and in this culture under the law, it constituted a rebellion punishable by death. Jesus' audience would have been stunned by the scandalous demands of the first son and even more stunned by the love of the father at every turn.

They would have been even more stunned that the father did not judge that son like his other son did. After all, the first son had rebelled and deserved punishment.

Instead, the father gives the inheritance, receives his son back in an embrace of love, and restores the son completely. What kind of a father is this? This is God, your Father, as Jesus introduces Him. As He is meant to be known. As He had never been seen before. Perhaps we still haven't gotten it. Is this the Father you have known? This is the Father who knows you fully and loves you completely.

You might take a moment to compare the story of the Prodigal Son with the story of the children of Israel in Exodus 19. In the Exodus 19 story, they leave slavery in Egypt to be led to be united in a Kingdom of face-to-face communion with the Father as priests. At Mount Sinai He directs them all to prepare for three days and come to the boundary line at the base of the mountain. When they hear the trumpet they are to "come up" to the Lord.

But the spectacle of meeting God is so fearful to them that even when the sound of the horn grows louder and louder, nobody moves. Though in Exodus 20:20 Moses tries to tell them that God is testing them, they demand that God speak with them no more, but delegate Moses to talk to God alone. Because the children of Israel didn't know how good God was, they couldn't conceive of being any more than the slaves they had been.

In the same way, the first prodigal in Jesus' story can't conceive of being received as a son, so the best he hopes for is as a slave. The lesson is this. Without a revelation of the goodness of God, the fear of the Lord will keep you from experiencing the presence of the Lord.

Thankfully, Hebrews 12 says that we are not at that mountain any longer, but we have now come to Mount Zion, to a good Father, and a joyful celebration of a new covenant. This covenant of union with you was His desire from the foundation of the world.

REFLECT ON THESE QUESTIONS

1. After studying this story in *The Forgotten Way*, what is the part of the Prodigal Son story that impacts you the most right now?

_____

_____

2. Has there ever been a time in your life when you wanted to or tried to be separated from God?

_____

_____

3. Which of the two sons do you identify with more? The one who runs after the world, or the one who judges those who run after the world?

_____

_____

4. Describe a time in your life when you've experienced the grace of God.

_____

_____

5. Describe a time in your life when you experienced the correction of God.

_____

_____

ACTIVATION

Being a child of the Father is reinforced by acknowledging it from the abundance of your heart. That means using your voice. Take some time by yourself and speak out loud saying, "Thank you, Father, for making me your child. I'm no longer a slave to fear. I am a child of God." It's important to understand that you actually have the ability to speak words of life or death to yourself. You are your own greatest encourager or discourager. And your encouragement begins with a revelation of your Father's love for you. This simple declaration dissolves your allegiance to a life shaped by fear and acknowledges your trust in the love of your Father.

SCRIPTURES AND REFLECTIONS FROM THE MEDITATION

1. **Luke 15:31-32** "My son," the father said, "you are always with me, and everything I have is yours. But we had to celebrate and be glad, because this

brother of yours was dead and is alive again; he was lost and is found." ***1 John 4:19*** *We love, because He first loved us.*

When the son crests the hill in the distance, the father runs toward him. Even before the son can get his rehearsed repentance speech out of his mouth, the father declares him restored. That's what your heavenly Father is like. Your behavior cannot manipulate God or dictate to Him whether He loves you or not. See your Father and see yourself. As you behold how loved you are by Him, you will understand what it means to love.

Your love for your Father will never be greater than your perception of how loved you are *by* your Father. When you see how loved you really are, your heart will respond, for even the love you have for Him is a gift of love from Him. He has fully supplied to you all the love you need, in Himself.

2. ***John 5:22*** ESV *The Father judges no one, but has given all judgment to the Son.*

So is the Son going to judge you? Though He certainly has the power to, this is what He said a few verses later: ***John 5:45*** *Do not think that I will accuse you before the Father; the one who accuses you is Moses, in whom you have set your hope.*

The law of Moses (as well as all systems of the world) unveil our sinfulness but have no power to do anything about it. Jesus reveals His heart toward us in that He has not come to accuse us, but to find and save us. This is the Father's heart.

John 3:17-18 *For God did not send the Son into the world to judge the world, but that the world might be saved through Him. He who believes in Him is not judged; he who does not believe has been judged already, because he has not believed in the name of the only begotten Son of God.*

Does condemnation exist for you? Yes, but its source is not God. Condemnation is from the accuser and from yourself, and it began at the fall. Do you remember what God asked Adam? *Who told you that you were naked?* They had always been naked and without shame because God did not judge the nakedness of His creation. We live under the weight of our own condemnation, and in condemning one another we condemn ourselves. But neither the Father nor the Son condemn you, for you are in Christ and He in you.

Romans 8:1-4 Therefore there is now no condemnation for those who are in Christ Jesus. For the law of the Spirit of life in Christ Jesus has set you free from the law of sin and of death. For what the Law could not do, weak as it was through the flesh, God did: sending His own Son in the likeness of sinful flesh and as an offering for sin, He condemned sin in the flesh, so that the requirement of the Law might be fulfilled in us.

You are legally obligated to be free, in Him. We are all legalists as such, and our liberation in Christ is our new law.

3. *Romans 5:20 The Law came in so that the transgression would increase; but where sin increased, grace abounded all the more so that as sin reigned in death, even so grace would reign through righteousness to eternal life through Jesus Christ our Lord.*

4. *Hebrews 8:7 NIV For if there had been nothing wrong with that first covenant* (the law of Moses) *no place would have been sought for another* (the law of grace in Christ's death and resurrection). *Hebrews 7:18-19 NIV The former regulation* (the law of Moses) *is set aside* (cancelled) *because it was weak and useless* (for the law made nothing perfect*) and a better hope is introduced* (the new law of grace) *by which we draw near to God* (know Him). *Hebrews 8:13 NIV By calling this covenant "new" he has made the first one* (the law of Moses) *obsolete. Romans 8:1-3 Therefore there is now no condemnation for those who are in Christ Jesus, because through Christ Jesus the law of the Spirit who gives life* (through grace) *has set you free from the law of sin and death. For what the law was powerless to do because it was weakened by the flesh, God did by sending his own Son in the likeness of sinful flesh to be a sin offering. And so he condemned sin in the flesh in order that the righteous requirement of the law might be fully met.*

The fulfillment of the law is grace in Christ. The law showed the world how powerless we are to attain righteousness through a system of rules and sacrifices—these only trap us in a never-ending cycle of failure. But in Christ we are free from the law of sin and death.

5. *Hebrews 12:6 NIV The Lord disciplines the one he loves, and he chastens everyone he accepts as his son.*

6. *Jeremiah 1:5 Before I formed you in the womb I knew you.*

Your Father has known you far longer than you can imagine. You existed in Him before you were ever formed in flesh. What did He think of when He dreamed of you? It was perfect, good, pure, a righteous reflection of His own holiness. The One who knew you before you could be known, is the only One qualified to define you. He truly knows you better than you know yourself. See now what He sees, for you are in Christ, and Christ is in you.

7. *Luke 11:34 The eye is the lamp of the body; when your eye is clear, your whole body also is full of light, but when it* (your perception) *is bad, your body also is full of darkness.* Your beliefs and perceptions determine your earthly experience, as we will see in greater depth later.

8. *1 Samuel 12:22 For the Lord will not abandon His people on account of His great name, because the Lord has been pleased to make you a people for Himself.*

Your Father's heart has always been for you and not against you. His promise silences a deep fear in us that we could be left alone, lost, or forgotten. The word for *name* in Hebrew means much more than something to be called. It speaks of identity and nature. Because of who He is, because of the very essence of His nature, He will not abandon you. That is the relentless affection of your Father.

Psalm 136:1-5 Give thanks to the Lord, for He is good, For His lovingkindness is everlasting. Give thanks to the God of gods, For His lovingkindness is everlasting. Give thanks to the Lord of lords, For His lovingkindness is everlasting. To Him who alone does great wonders, For His lovingkindness is everlasting. To Him who made the heavens with skill, For His lovingkindness is everlasting.

A revelation of your Father's goodness will generate gratitude. King David writes in the Psalms a repeated phrase that was a foreign and unfolding concept in the Old Testament: that God would care to express love, that He would be kind, and that He is good. These were concepts that David understood because his heart was awakening to its authentic identity. He was a man after God's own heart. In spite of his sins and failures, he could find grace and intimacy in the presence of God. David perceived the goodness of God in ways that many of us, thousands of years later, struggle to see.

9. *Psalm 91:1-2* NIV *He who dwells in the shelter of the Most High will abide in the shadow of the Almighty. I will say of the Lord, "He is my refuge, my fortress, my God, in whom I trust."*

Trust is born out of union and intimacy. How do you trust God? Let go of all judgment, all offense, all grievance. These are not what define you. You are who your Father says you are.

You have come to the end of the Meditations 1 through 3 which represent who your Father is in <u>Truth</u>.

Read and consider the first declaration

THE TRUTH

THE FIRST DECLARATION
Meditations 1-3

God is infinitely good, *far more loving and gentle and kind to His children than any earthly mother or father imaginable.* ***God is infinitely complete***; *nothing can threaten or disturb Him. Nothing can be taken away from Him, making Him less than complete, nor added to Him who is already complete.*

FOUR

THE STORY OF YOU

"Life comes only through Christ—there is no other way. He alone is the Truth, the Way, the Life. No man may know the Father but by Him. He is the only path."

"Rejoice in the certainty of your own salvation through the unshakable power of Yeshua who has forever, with far more authority and power than the first Adam or the serpent, restored you."

THE TALE OF TWO ADAMS AND YOU

The Father is great, infinite, and complete. Adam, though not God, was made in the image and likeness of God who glorified His identity in him. It is often said that Adam was made in the image of God but you are made in the image of Adam, bearing the weight of Adam's fall.

But you're no longer under the curse of the first Adam. Jesus, the second Adam, is called the chief cornerstone, and the principle of the cornerstone was that every stone fashioned for a house was made in the likeness of that perfect template. You are now made in His likeness. Adam's fall no longer defines you.

Before the fall, Adam and Eve experienced communion with God without any hindrance. There was no judgment, no shame, no lack. The lie of the serpent deceived them into believing that God was withholding something from them and they became confused about their own identity. In taking matters into their own hands to correct the problem, they were saying in their hearts to God, "Not Your will but ours."

It's nearly impossible to conceive of a world without judgment, because that's all we have known. Every one of us have experienced judgment, guilt, and shame and so tasted of the fruit of the fall. Adam's sin condemned us all. We were born into a world filled with offense, ego, and grievance—blind to who we were originally created to be.

But Jesus, the anointed One, stood in our place as the last Adam and in the garden, declares on our behalf, "Not My will but Yours be done." Jesus is crucified by His own creation and His response is grace. The resurrection now affirms your innocence in Him.

You are now restored in the image and likeness of your Father with unhindered reconciliation, glorified with Christ in His image once again. Rejoice today in the certainty of Jesus's victorious salvation, because His redemption is more powerful than Adam's sin. Just as Jesus declared Himself to be the light of the world, so now He has imparted that same identity to you.

Let all doubt and confusion fall away as you taste and see that your Father is good. As you begin to see Him in His glory, goodness, and grace, you will begin to know who you truly are.

You are not forsaken. You are eternally loved by a good Father who is glorified by making you in His likeness once more.

REFLECT ON THESE QUESTIONS

1. Do you have any fears that cause you to question your salvation? What are they?

_____

_____

2. What is one key lesson you have learned from the story of two Adams and you?

_____

_____

3. Using your imagination, describe a world without judgment, guilt, or shame.

_____

_____

4. Who was more powerful in their affects upon the world—the first Adam who condemned all through one act of disobedience, or the last Adam, Jesus? How?

_____

_____

5. Being restored in Christ, in what ways do you now experience communion with your Father?

_____

_____

SCRIPTURES AND REFLECTIONS FROM THE MEDITATION

1. *Genesis 1:26-27* *Then God said, "Let Us make man in Our image, according to Our likeness; and let them rule over the fish of the sea and over the birds of the sky and over the cattle and over all the earth, and over every creeping thing that creeps on the earth." God created man in His own image, in the image of God He created him; male and female He created them.* *Genesis 2:7* *Then the Lord God formed man from the dust of the ground, and breathed into his nostrils the breath of life.*

We are made in the likeness of God. In breathing life into Adam, God also infused him with His identity. There are only two times in the Scriptures where it is said that God breathed on man. The first is here in Genesis, and the second is in John 20:22 after the resurrection of Christ. There, He breathes upon the disciples and says, "Receive the Holy Spirit." The first breath infused us with the identity of the Holy Spirit of God. The second does no less. His breath restored us to the deepest possible intimacy with our Father.

In essence, the One who created mankind in the beginning came once more to recreate you through His own death and resurrection. What a powerful story.

2. *John 12:28 "Father, glorify Your name."* Then a voice came out of heaven: "I have both glorified it, and will glorify it again." *Luke 3:38 Adam, the son of God.*

This context of Adam being called a son of God beautifully compares that first Adam with Jesus, who is called the last Adam in 1 Corinthians 15:45. Adam failed to resist the tempter in the garden, but Jesus successfully resisted the tempter in the wilderness. Just as Adam's failure was imparted to you, so now Christ's victory is yours as well. Mankind's broken communion with the Father has been restored in the mystery of the reconciliation of Jesus Christ.

3. *John 1:1-4 In the beginning was the Word, and the Word was with God, and the Word was God. He was in the beginning with God. All things came into being through Him, and apart from Him nothing came into being that has come into being. In Him was life, and the life was the Light of men.*

It might seem perplexing to reference this verse at this point in the study, but see here that John begins his account of Jesus with a parallel to the story of Creation. In Genesis 1 God makes us in His likeness, yet here in John 1 something important is clarified: Christ was there at the beginning, doing the creating. So to be made in the likeness of God is to be made in the likeness of Jesus. In as much, you have been remade in that same likeness through Jesus. Think about this.

The image you're created in is God in Christ Jesus, for you are made in the image and likeness of the Word, and the Word is who created you. Jesus demonstrates to us the most authentic way to be human. In His likeness you are intelligent, relational, creative, eternal, glorified, spiritual. His life is our life, and His light is our light. You are not God, and He is not you. But you are *in* Him, and He is *in* you. This beautiful mystery of union is the basis of your identity.

4. *1 John 1:5 God is Light, and in Him there is no darkness at all.*

5. *Genesis 3:9-13* Then the Lord God called to the man, and said to him, "Where are you?" He said, "I heard the sound of You in the garden,

and I was afraid because I was naked; so I hid myself." And He said, "Who told you that you were naked? Have you eaten from the tree of which I commanded you not to eat?" The man said, "The woman whom You gave to be with me, she gave me from the tree, and I ate." Then the Lord God said to the woman, "What is this you have done?" And the woman said, "The serpent deceived me, and I ate."

Fear of our own shame (self-judgment) causes us to judge others. This knowledge of good and evil is the fruit of the fall, and we eat it every day. When we choose fear over love, we go blind to authentic identity—ours and everyone else's. In Jesus you are restored to your original identity. That is who you are and how deeply you are loved by your Father.

6. ***John 1:4-5*** NIV *In him was life, and that life was the light of all mankind. The light shines in the darkness, and the darkness has not overcome it.*

The contrast between dark and light is clear as John describes the confused weakness of darkness and the overpowering invasion of light. The illusion that darkness has substance is only convincing if no light is present. But in truth, the light has come into all darkness, not just into a small corner of it, not just in half the atoms or half of the world. The darkness has not overcome it, anywhere. God is not only partially victorious. Neither is His Son.

7. ***John 12:28*** *"Father, glorify Your name." Then a voice came out of heaven: "I have both glorified it, and will glorify it again."*

8. ***Psalm 22:1*** *My God, my God, why have You forsaken me?* ***Matthew 27:46*** *About the ninth hour Jesus cried out with a loud voice, saying, "Eli, Eli, lama sabachthani?" that is, "My God, My God, why have You forsaken Me?"*

9. ***John 19:30*** *Therefore when Jesus had received the sour wine, He said, "It is finished!" And He bowed His head and gave up His spirit.*

10. ***Romans 8:1-2*** *Therefore there is now no condemnation for those who are in Christ Jesus. For the law of the Spirit of life in Christ Jesus has set you free from the law of sin and of death.*

There has been much division in the church over the question of whether we're under law or under grace. But this doesn't need to be so, because as Paul understood it here, we are clearly still under law, just not the *old* law. Every student of law understands the concept of an overturned law. When a new law overturns an old one, the new law becomes the standard. The old standard is no longer legal or relevant.

In Christ there is a new law, and it's called "the law of the Spirit of life in Christ." The result of this is that you are at a place of perfect liberty; that is what grace is. The Spirit of God has unveiled a limitless horizon before you. He has empowered you to dream and to do according to the infinite ability of an absolutely good Father. Now, the most authentic "legalists" are the ones who recognize their true freedom. Grace has become the higher law.

11. *Isaiah 9:2 The people who walk in darkness Will see a great light; Those who live in a dark land, The light will shine on them.* *John 8:12 I am the Light of the world.* *Matthew 5:14 You are the light of the world.*

Who is the "you" in that last verse? Meditate on the powerful beauty of this mystery. What does it mean to be the light of the world? This can only be understood when you know that all distance and separation that once existed between you and Christ has been eliminated.

12. *John 12:28 "Father, glorify Your name." Then a voice came out of heaven: "I have both glorified it, and will glorify it again."* *Romans 3:23-24 For all have sinned and fallen short of the glory of God, being justified as a gift by His grace through the redemption which is in Christ Jesus.*

Have you ever read those three verses together? You were made to shine with the glory of God, but sin created the darkness of separation between you and Him. But the Father planned to glorify His identity once more through the death and resurrection of the second Adam, and Paul makes it clear in Romans.

Most of the time, Romans 3:23 is quoted all by itself, giving the impression that the end of the verse is the end of the thought. But this isn't the case. This Scripture doesn't make the case for your guilt, but for your innocence. You no longer fall short of the glory of God in Christ. He has now glorified His name again in you. Now Jesus's prayer begins to make much more sense.

John 17:22-23 The glory which You have given Me I have given to them, that they may be one, just as We are one; I in them and You in Me, that they may be perfected in unity, so that the world may know that You sent Me, and loved them, even as You have loved Me.

Without Him, you would most certainly be nothing. Thankfully you are not without Him. You began in the mind and heart of God. So before you can discover who you truly are, turn your affection to the origin of your identity and see your Father as He truly is. Whatever has your positive attention also has your affection, and in encountering your Father, you will discover an affirming revelation of yourself. You were created to radiate the goodness of God.

13. ***Romans 5:17-18, 20*** *For if by the transgression of the one, death reigned through the one, much more those who receive the abundance of grace and of the gift of righteousness will reign in life through the One, Jesus Christ. So then as through one transgression there resulted condemnation to all men, even so through one act of righteousness there resulted justification of life to all men . . . The Law came in so that the transgression would increase; but where sin increased, grace abounded all the more.*

Whatever Adam's sin did to condemn you, Jesus's grace has done much more. This is a great and wonderful mystery. You haven't outrun or run out of the grace of God. Sin will never exhaust the righteousness of truth, for truth is not an opinion of man. Truth is the person of Jesus Christ.

14. ***1 Corinthians 13:12*** *For now we see in a mirror dimly, but then face to face; now I know in part, but then I will know fully just as I also have been fully known.*

15. ***Ecclesiastes 3:11*** *He has made everything appropriate in its time. He has also set eternity in their heart, yet so that man will not find out the work which God has done from the beginning even to the end.* ***Isaiah 57:15*** ESV *For thus says the One who is high and lifted up, who inhabits eternity, whose name is Holy: "I dwell in the high and holy place, and also with him who is of a contrite and lowly spirit, to revive the spirit of the lowly, and to revive the heart of the contrite."*

Some say God is outside of time but can see the whole spectrum from beginning to end. Some say God operates within time and limits Himself so that He doesn't see what is going to happen, yet still remains involved. Both possibilities may have elements of truth.

But it is clear that God created all things, including time, and His eternal realm is not defined by the time He created. Before there was time, there was God: *2 Timothy 1:9* NIV *He has saved us and called us to a holy life—not because of anything we have done but because of his own purpose and grace. This grace was given us in Christ Jesus before the beginning of time.* Time is a beautiful creation that gives us the opportunity to observe and understand the good work that our Father is doing within us, for He has never stopped creating. We will forever be awakening to what has always been, and what has always been is love.

16. *Ephesians 1:4* NIV *For he chose us in him before the creation of the world to be holy and blameless in his sight. In love he predestined us for adoption to sonship through Jesus Christ, in accordance with his pleasure and will—to the praise of his glorious grace, which he has freely given us in the One he loves.*

God Himself is your point of origin. You began in His heart and mind, by His sovereign will. Even before the foundation or fall of the world, He saw you as His son, His daughter, the incarnation of the Godhead on earth as it is in heaven.

17. *Psalm 22:24, 31* NIV *For he has not despised or scorned the suffering of the afflicted one; he has not hidden his face from him but has listened to his cry for help. They will proclaim his righteousness, declaring to a people yet unborn: He has done it!*

FIVE

SEEING WHO YOU ARE

*When you dare believe the truth of who you are now, you
will no longer cling to all manner of vain imaginations
of what you think this world offers.*

WHO AM I?

Now reconciled to your Father, see that there is no room for fear of punishment, but only delight and confidence in this relationship. How do you believe your Father sees you? If you only see yourself through the eyes of judgment, then you feel guilt and shame and, in blindness, see others the same.

Jesus went to unimaginable lengths to demonstrate to the world how the Father loves, and now invites you to awaken and live as reconciled. Don't be consumed with becoming. Simply be. Being seated with Christ in heavenly places isn't a place of apathy, but rather true rest and peace.

Paul, a man who struggled just like us, wrote about an understanding of being in Christ. He understood that the old creature was racked with guilt and shame, but you are now a new creation where old things have passed away and all things have become new. Your old identity is now as dead as Adam. Your true identity is now as alive as Christ.

Only the old mind clings to an old identity, filled with deception. Your journey is to let go of your identification with the old and replace it with what the Father says is true about you.

This is the clarity that the renewed mind brings. Today, believe in the name of Jesus. Receive His grace by realizing that while you were blinded by sin and separation, He reconciled you to Himself. While every other identity can be shaken by circumstances in this life, the identity of being in Him can never be shaken. From that place in His identity, you can find peace in the midst of the storms of life.

Your brother, Paul, knew what it was like to be blind. He knew what it was like to be in a storm. He experienced the darkest corners of living, and found the peace he carried in Jesus to be far more powerful than any circumstance around him. May you daily discover the joy of salvation.

REFLECT ON THESE QUESTIONS

1. How do you believe your Father sees you right now?

_____

_____

2. Why do you think it is so easy for us to go blind to who we truly are?

_____

_____

3. Have you ever thought of yourself as perfect and holy? Describe yourself this way.

_____

_____

4. What do you think it means to be seated with Christ in heavenly places?

_____

_____

5. Are you aware of being "in Christ" right now?

_____

_____

ACTIVATION

Take a moment to journal and describe two people you admire and know personally. Describe three specific traits of each person that you admire, giving as much detail as you can. Notice how the goodness you see and consider in another person causes you to want to draw close to them. Could it be that the reason many people don't want to know God is that we haven't revealed His goodness? Write down some practical ways you can reveal the goodness of the Father to others.

SCRIPTURES AND REFLECTIONS FROM THE MEDITATION

1. *1 Corinthians 6:19 Do you not know that your body is a temple of the Holy Spirit who is in you, whom you have from God, and that you are not your own?*

There is a difference between the body and the Spirit. Your body is a temple, but *only* a temple. It is not who you are. It is merely a costume, a vessel that contains the eternal you. So treat it with great respect, but do not mistake it for more than it is. It is a beautiful but decaying vessel. Paul asks his question rhetorically: Isn't it really self-evident that we are created to be the dwelling place of God? Keep in mind that the churches Paul is writing to had no New Testament and little or no access to Old Testament Scriptures. They had nothing but the gospel that Paul shared with them and the indwelling power of the Holy Spirit. Yet Paul finds it hard to believe that they don't understand their union with God in Christ by the power of the Holy Spirit. I wonder if Paul would be just as surprised by our lack of belief today.

2. *Matthew 5:48 Therefore you are to be perfect, as your heavenly Father is perfect. 1 John 4:17 As He is, so also are we in this world.*

The Greek word for "be" (*Esomai*) here is different than the word "become" (*Ginomai*). *Esomai* is not an assignment commanding you to strive to become something. It's a prophetic revelation of your present identity. This is Jesus's declaration of Christ in you, the hope of glory. *Perfect* and *holy* is who you are right now. For you are as He is.

2 Corinthians 5:21 *He made Him who knew no sin to be sin on our behalf, so that we might become the righteousness of God in Him.*

Our blindness to how our Father sees us keeps us in a behavioral cycle of consistent failure. Holiness is the natural response of a heart at rest in the grace of God. Righteousness is not something you become. It is who you are.

3. **Galatians 2:20** *I have been crucified with Christ; and it is no longer I who live, but Christ lives in me; and the life which I now live in the flesh I live by faith in the Son of God, who loved me and gave Himself up for me.*

Paul was making a personal application (I myself have been crucified) to unveil a divine revelation of his own identity. To receive what God says about you means you have to be willing to listen to God speak about you in this way. It's as if Paul heard Jesus say, *You have been crucified with me, and it is no longer you who live, but I who live in you; and the life you now live in the flesh you live by faith in me, who loves you and gave myself for you.*

4. **Ephesians 2:4-6** *God, being rich in mercy, because of His great love with which He loved us, even when we were dead in our transgressions, made us alive together with Christ (by grace you have been saved), and raised us up with Him, and seated us with Him in the heavenly places in Christ Jesus.*

The result of your co-crucifixion and co-resurrection is that you are currently, right now, present in this world of form and dimension of time, and simultaneously present in the dimension of eternity. It's far too grand for our minds to grasp as long as we believe that all we see is all there is. But our spirits know far more truth than our minds currently understand.

5. **Romans 8:29-30** *For those whom He foreknew, He also predestined to become conformed to the image of His Son, so that He would be the firstborn among many brethren; and these whom He predestined, He also called; and these whom He called, He also justified; and these whom He justified, He also glorified.*

6. *1 Timothy 1:15-16* *It is a trustworthy statement, deserving full acceptance, that Christ Jesus came into the world to save sinners, among whom I am foremost of all. Yet for this reason I found mercy, so that in me as the foremost, Jesus Christ might demonstrate His perfect patience as an example for those who would believe in Him for eternal life.*

Philippians 3:8-15 *More than that, I count all things to be loss in view of the surpassing value of knowing Christ Jesus my Lord . . . so that I may gain Christ, and may be found in Him, not having a righteousness of my own derived from the Law, but that which is through faith in Christ, the righteousness which comes from God on the basis of faith, that I may know Him and the power of His resurrection and the fellowship of His sufferings, being conformed to His death; in order that I may attain to the resurrection from the dead. Not that I have already obtained it or have already become perfect (fully experienced the perfection of union in Christ in this life,) but I press on so that I may lay hold of that for which also I was laid hold of by Christ Jesus. Brethren, I do not regard myself as having laid hold of it yet; but one thing I do: forgetting what lies behind and reaching forward to what lies ahead, I press on toward the goal for the prize of the upward call of God in Christ Jesus. Let us therefore, as many as are perfect, have this attitude.*

1 Corinthians 12:7-8 *Because of the surpassing greatness of the revelations, for this reason, to keep me from exalting myself, there was given me a thorn in the flesh, a messenger of Satan to torment me—to keep me from exalting myself! Concerning this I implored the Lord three times that it might leave me. And He has said to me, "My grace is sufficient for you, for power is perfected in weakness."*

7. *2 Corinthians 5:17* *Therefore if anyone is in Christ, he is a new creature; the old things passed away; behold, new things have come.*

The Greek word translated "creature" here is *kitisis*, which simply means "creation." To make something new is not like fixing something that was broken, but rather like making something for the very first time, as if the broken had never even existed. Only one who is the master of time could do such a thing. *Romans 8:1* *Therefore there is now no condemnation for those who are in Christ Jesus. Colossians 2:10 In Him you have been made complete.*

Is there any question of who you are in Christ? Thus the words of Jesus from the cross: *It is finished!*

8. *2 Corinthians 4:7* NIV *But we have this treasure in jars of clay, to show that this all-surpassing power is from God and not from us.* *2 Corinthians 5:1* ESV *For we know that if the tent that is our earthly home is destroyed, we have a building from God, a house not made with hands, eternal in the heavens.* *2 Corinthians 4:18* NIV *So we fix our eyes* (perception) *not on what is seen, but on what is unseen, since what is seen is temporary* (including the body you see) *but what is unseen is eternal* (your true spiritual self). *2 Corinthians 5:16 Therefore from now on we recognize no one according to the flesh; even though we have known Christ according to the flesh, yet now we know Him in this way no longer.*

Do you ever think about your spirit? Do you know that you are a spiritual being? Try something today: think of the body as a costume we are all wearing. Ignore everybody's costume and ask your Father to reveal to you what He believes about them. Each person is a much-loved child of God made in His image and likeness. Remember, that is who you are too.

9. *James 2:19 You believe that God is one. You do well; the demons also believe, and shudder.*

10. *2 Timothy 3:5 For men will be lovers of self . . . holding to a form of godliness, although they have denied its power.*

11. *Colossians 2:8 See to it that no one takes you captive through philosophy and empty deception, according to the tradition of men, according to the elementary principles of the world, rather than according to Christ.*

12. *Ephesians 2:8 For by grace you have been saved through faith; and that not of yourselves, it is the gift of God. Hebrews 11:1-3 Now faith is the assurance* (substance) *of things hoped for, the conviction* (evidence) *of things not seen . . . By faith we understand that the worlds were prepared by the word of God, so that what is seen was not made out of things which are visible.*

In Western culture, we protect ourselves from deception by putting our faith only in that which we first understand. But there are things in Christ that require faith before we can understand. Even then, your spirit knows what your mind can't yet fully grasp. Surrendering what you think you know, in order to be who you truly are (loved, whole, secure, complete, at rest, in him), requires the very faith that God Himself freely gives you.

13. *Acts 26:17-18 I am sending you to open their eyes so that they may turn from darkness to light and from the dominion of Satan to God, that they may receive forgiveness of sins and an inheritance among those who have been sanctified by faith in Me.*

Our brother Paul was confronted by the Light, left in the tomb of his own blindness for three days, then commissioned to turn mankind from darkness to light. How much more can a person be identified with the mission of Christ?

14. *John 5:22 ESV The Father judges no one but has given all judgment to the Son. Matthew 7:1 Do not judge so that you will not be judged. John 5:45 Do not think that I will accuse you before the Father; the one who accuses you is Moses, in whom you have set your hope.*

SIX

THE GREAT MYSTERY

There is no greater gift you can possibly hope for or receive in this life than to subjectively know and abide in Yeshua's staggering declaration of who you are.

ONE

We have all heard of the Trinity, a beautiful mystery that defies human logic and reason. Where we are only beginning to understand time, progression, space, distance, substance, and form, God hints at a realm beyond this where a singular union is possible. The Oneness of Jesus and the Father and the Holy Spirit is a union of self-giving love.

Jesus' prayer in John 17 is that we would live as one in the same way He and the Father are One. What a beautiful picture of grace and communion that is only hinted at in the most loving marriage between two and the life that union births.

Another clear picture of this is found in the nature of vines and branches grafted into a root system that gives life. The nature of this union brings forth life and the Father prunes anything in you that does not bear fruit, so that life and love can flow through you as the body of Christ here on earth. What a loving Father, then!

In Jesus, we now have been grafted into the relationship of the Trinity, three but One at the same time. This perspective of self-giving love is not limited to God alone, but is also to be lived out among us who are created in His image and likeness.

Jesus' radical statement that you are in Him and He is in you defies logic, because it means that there is no separation between you and Him. You are one, even as He and the Father are one. In this way, He has given you the same glory that He has in the Father.

Begin now to see this glorious union which can only be known with the help of the Spirit of Truth, as Jesus said.

REFLECT ON THESE QUESTIONS

1. If you are in Christ and He in you right now, as one, just as He is one with the Father, how does that change the way you see yourself?

_____

_____

2. How does that union change the way you see others?

_____

_____

3. How does that union affect the way you experience this life?

_____

_____

4. In unpacking the story of Superman, what childlike dreams were awakened within you?

_____

_____

ACTIVATION

Jesus said that you are in Him and He is in you at the same time. Lift up a glass of water or anything you drink. Imagine that the glass is you and the water is Jesus. You see that the water (Jesus) is in the glass (you). But can you also see that the glass is in the water?

No, not with earthly eyes. To see them in each other would be to see them as one, seamlessly integrated without separation. This is what He sees as He sees you. You are in Him and He is in you, as one.

As your mind is renewed to this awareness, your experience of life here on earth will be transformed. So then, be transformed by the renewing of your mind.

SCRIPTURES AND REFLECTIONS FROM THE MEDITATION

1. *1 John 5:7* KJV *For there are three that bear record in heaven, the Father, the Word, and the Holy Ghost: and these three are one.*

Jesus demonstrated what it truly means to be human. The relationship of love and trust that you have with your Father is possible because you are united by the power of the Spirit.

2. Quantum science is revealing a realm that defies the mechanical laws of Newtonian physics we all grew up understanding. Surely our children's children will have a much better understanding of nature than we do, even as we now have a better understanding than those who once believed the world was flat. In the quantum world, particles both exist as material, and don't, at the same time. They can be at two places at once, and they are not bound by space and time. This has been proven over and over, and yet no one knows how it works.

God consistently frustrates human wisdom that exalts itself apart from God. Trying to understand God fully through the lens of the physical world without the help of the Spirit (as science has tried to do for years) is like my dog trying to understand the internet. There are dimensions that we can't even begin to comprehend, and now even science is embracing the mystery of it all, in large part because of quantum physics. In fact, at times it seems that science is ahead of traditional religion when it comes to contemplating things like two things being one at the same time in the quantum realm.

3. *John 14:20* ESV *In that day you will know that I am in My Father, and you in Me, and I in you.*

Take a moment and consider the staggering implications of this statement. If you believe Jesus's words to be true, then the reality is both overwhelming and inevitable, and available for you to know now. God (Father, Son, Spirit) is fully resident and present within you now. The notion that "Christ lives in us" has perhaps been overstated to the point that we are desensitized to the truth of it. But how beautiful to know that we are not merely the expendable and deteriorating home of God. No, He is also the home we live within.

4. ***Matthew 25:40*** *Truly I say to you, to the extent that you did it to one of these brothers of Mine, even the least of them, you did it to Me.*

The least of them that Jesus was referring to were those considered sinners in His day. What we do to others, including outcasts and sinners, we are actually doing to Christ. So then, let us treat all of our brothers and sisters in this world as we would treat Christ. Jesus chooses the least to call His brothers. He puts no effort of theirs on display as qualification. It is not their badness on display but rather His goodness. Why are we so quick to look at our brothers and be angry at what they have or have not done? We judge those who offend us and our ego demands justice, but treating others as Christ is the beginning of being the light of the world.

5. ***John 17:3*** *This is eternal life, that they may know You, the only true God, and Jesus Christ whom You have sent.*

6. ***John 15:5-11*** *I am the vine, you are the branches; he who abides in Me and I in him, he bears much fruit, for apart from Me you can do nothing. If anyone does not abide in Me, he is thrown away as a branch and dries up; and they gather them, and cast them into the fire and they are burned.*

To the extent that you hold onto the perspective that you are separated from Him, you will find yourself in suffering.

If you abide in Me, and My words abide in you, ask whatever you wish, and it will be done for you.

It is in the context of being in Him that all things are possible.

My Father is glorified by this, that you bear much fruit, and so prove to be My disciples. Just as the Father has loved Me, I have also loved you; abide in My love. If you keep My commandments, you will abide in My love; just as I have kept My Father's commandments and abide in His love. These things

I have spoken to you so that My joy may be in you, and that your joy may be made full.

The fruit of the vine here is love. If you read these words and your heart isn't filled with love and joy, you missed the true message.

7. **Genesis 3:22-24** KJV *And the Lord God said, Behold, the man is become as one of us, to know good and evil: and now, lest he put forth his hand, and take also of the tree of life, and eat, and live for ever: Therefore the Lord God sent him forth from the garden of Eden.*

In the garden, the tree of life is seen as a source of eternal life for those who eat of its fruit. In the New Testament, Christ is the source of eternal life for all who believe. He is the tree of life. In **Psalm 34:8** we're encouraged to approach God in a radical way: *taste and see that the Lord is good.* Then in **John 6:56** Jesus makes a most shocking claim, establishing Himself as our tree of life. *He who eats My flesh and drinks My blood abides in Me, and I in him.*

If Jesus is the tree of life for us, and you are in Him, then who are you? You are the branches directly attached to the vine (the trunk and root system that sources life).

Ezekiel 47:12 *By the river on its bank, on one side and on the other, will grow all kinds of trees for food. Their leaves will not wither and their fruit will not fail. They will bear every month because their water flows from the sanctuary, and their fruit will be for food and their leaves for healing.*

Here's a verse about you. **Psalm 1:3** *He will be like a tree firmly planted by streams of water, Which yields its fruit in its season, And its leaf does not wither; And in whatever he does, he prospers.*

Finally in Revelation the tree of life appears again. Its function directly relates to Jesus's mandate to us to bring healing to the broken. **Revelation 12:22** *On either side of the river was the tree of life, bearing twelve kinds of fruit, yielding its fruit every month; and the leaves of the tree were for the healing of the nations.*

In Him, you are revealed as the tree of life for the nations. In you, He is revealed as the ultimate Savior.

8. **Ephesians 5:28-32** ESV *In the same way husbands should love their wives as their own bodies. He who loves his wife loves himself. For no one ever hated his own flesh, but nourishes and cherishes it, just as Christ does*

THE FORGOTTEN WAY | STUDY GUIDE

the church, because we are members of his body. "Therefore a man shall leave his father and mother and hold fast to his wife, and the two shall become one flesh." This mystery is profound, and I am saying that it refers to Christ and the church.

While Paul's advice can be applied to marriage, that's not what he's really talking about. He's painting a picture of you and God in Christ. The intimacy of human marriage is a metaphor for your union with God. Christ loves you the way He loves Himself. Why? Because you are His body.

9. *John 17:22-23* ESV *The glory that you have given me I have given to them, that they may be one even as we are one, I in them and you in me, that they may become perfectly one, so that the world may know that you sent me and loved them even as you loved me.*

You carry the presence of the glorious One with and within you. Therefore you are, by association, glorious. It's illogical to claim that Jesus lives within you and at the same time claim that you are not glorious. When understood, there's no pride in that reality. Just gratitude.

10. *Romans 8:29-30* *For those whom He foreknew, He also predestined to become conformed to the image of His Son, so that He would be the firstborn among many brethren; and these whom He predestined, He also called; and these whom He called, He also justified; and these whom He justified, He also glorified.*

This can be difficult to understand unless you (a) realize that you are joined together with Christ and (b) see yourself from an eternal perspective. Being glorified was your destiny before the invention of time itself. It has been thought that being glorified is impossible without being sanctified (declared holy). But what if you've already been sanctified?

John 17:19 *For their sakes I sanctify Myself, that they themselves also may be sanctified in truth.*

Apart from Jesus, your sanctification is impossible. Your union with righteousness Himself overcomes your sin nature by grace. For this reason, Paul can say with confidence in *2 Corinthians 5:21* *He made Him who knew no sin to be sin on our behalf, so that we might become the righteousness of God in Him.*

SEVEN
SONS AND DAUGHTERS OF THE FATHER

*Because you are in Christ and He in you, you, too, are
the child of Yeshua's Father.*

BEING A CHILD

What an indescribable honor, to be the son and daughter of a good Father who cannot be threatened. There are many who play the role of a father in this life, and knowing who they are could mean the difference between a child growing up having a clear picture of our true "Father" who does not condemn, or of a Father who is distant, even cruel.

How tragic it is when an earthly father, in his blindness, doesn't realize that his primary role is to represent the Father to his children. To represent the heart of the Father we must see the Father as He is, because we reflect what we behold. Today, purpose in your heart to give attention to seeing your Father as He is. Even if you don't understand where to begin, the Spirit of Truth will respond lovingly to your intention and provide a way to see that desire fulfilled in a way that's unique to you. To see the Father is to be drawn into the experience of knowing the Father. And it is in the knowing Him that we discover who we truly are.

Being a child of the Father, we can know Jesus, who is called the firstborn of many brothers and sisters. Though the physical world and the roles we play here are so prominent in our vision and experience, inside we know there is more, even if we don't understand it. The truth is that a part of us knows far more than our minds show us. The eternal you is aware of a realm beyond what you see with your eyes. In that realm and in this, you are the son, the daughter, of God, as it is written.

REFLECT ON THESE QUESTIONS

1. What is your biggest challenge to seeing God as your Father?

_____

_____

2. What does it mean to be a son or daughter of God, even as Jesus, your brother, is?

_____

_____

3. What do you think would be some of the benefits to being a child of the Father?

_____

_____

4. In what ways do you reflect the heart of the Father?

_____

_____

SCRIPTURES AND REFLECTIONS FROM THE MEDITATION

1. *Galatians 3:26 For you are all sons* (and daughters) *of God though faith in Christ.* *Galatians 4:6* NIV *Because you are his sons* (and daughters), *God sent forth the Spirit of his Son into our hearts, the Spirit who cries out, "Abba, Father!"* *Romans 8:19* NIV *For the creation waits in eager expectation for the children of God to be revealed.*

Creation is literally waiting for us to awaken to who we really are.

2. *Matthew 23:9 Do not call anyone on earth your father; for One is your Father, He who is in heaven.*

As you continue to study the Scriptures, read them from a perspective of being "in Him." You'll begin to realize that the mysteries and hard sayings of the Bible are clarified. Your earthly father may have failed you, but have no fear, for he is not your Father in Christ. There is no need to make God in his image.

3. *Luke 14:26 If anyone comes to Me, and does not hate his own father and mother and wife and children and brothers and sisters, yes, and even his own life, he cannot be My disciple.*

In Christ, you're not rejecting anyone. If the teachings of Jesus could be summed up in a single phrase, it would be, "Let go." Surrender who you think you are so that you might be who you truly are.

4. *Romans 8:29 For those whom He foreknew, He also predestined to become conformed to the image of His Son, so that He would be the firstborn among many brethren.*

THE TRUTH: SUMMARY

In this first section we have entered seven meditations on the simplest *Truth* about who the *Father* is and who *you* are, as the son or the daughter of the Father through Yeshua.

These constitute the first and second declarations of The Forgotten Way.

THE FIRST DECLARATION
Meditations 1-3

God is infinitely good*, far more loving and gentle and kind to His children than any earthly mother or father imaginable. **God is infinitely complete***; *nothing can threaten or disturb Him. Nothing can be taken away from Him, making Him less than complete, nor added to Him who is already complete.*

THE SECOND DECLARATION
Mediations 4-7

You are remade in the likeness and glory of your Father*, finite yet already complete in union with Yeshua—you in Him and He in you, risen with Him and seated in heavenly places. Nothing can separate you from His love.*

II

THE WAY

Yeshua made it plain: *I am the Way, the Truth and the Life.*

In the second section, we will enter seven meditations on the *Way* of Yeshua, which is, first, to *see* who you are in the eternal realm of the Father's presence now at hand (meditations 8-11) by, second, *surrendering* all other identities (meditations 12-14).

These constitute the third and fourth declarations of The Forgotten Way.

THE THIRD DECLARATION

Your journey now is to <u>see</u> who you truly are, *for you are the light of the world, the son or the daughter of your Father, a new creature flowing with more beauty and power than you have dared imagine possible.*

THE FOURTH DECLARATION

You will only see who you are and thus be who you are as you surrender your attachment to all other identities, *which are like gods of a lesser power that block your vision of your true identity and keep you in darkness.*

EIGHT

THE TALE OF TWO KINGDOMS

There are two kingdoms now to see, though fully integrated and both good: the kingdom of the eternal realm, and the kingdom of all that perishes and returns to dust.

BEING AWARE OF THE ETERNAL

The two kingdoms are the kingdom of heaven, of Jesus, of Spirit, and the system of the world which is passing away. Eternal life is to recognize that time has no restraint or ability to overpower Spirit. Spirit by Divine nature is anchored in eternity. So then, if eternal life is a dimension rather than a destination, then eternal life can be accessed now. Eternal life has already begun.

There has been much discussion on the meaning of the Greek word for eternal, *aeonios*. In some contexts it means age after age, in the continuing of time. But time, which we know is temporal and bound in form, is a difficult thing to grasp with the human mind. Regardless, Jesus specifically defines eternal life and He is our final authority. Hear Him again:

This is eternal (aeonios) life, that they may know (experience) You, the only true God, and Jesus Christ whom You have sent. Clearly, Jesus' explicit expression of eternal life is a quality of relationship in Him who brings us into a present knowledge and experience of God, our Father.

In the same way, when Jesus declared that the Kingdom of heaven is within and among us, He was extending an invitation to step into a realm that was already present. He was building a bridge of reconciliation between us and our origin, source, purpose, our Father. In revealing the Kingdom filled with love, joy, and peace, He made clear what we were blinded to. That love, joy, and peace is both where we're from and who we are, because it is our Father who defines these things and who remade us in His image and likeness through the death and resurrection of Christ.

It is important to realize that the temporal world is a creation of God, and it is beautiful. To elevate the realm of Spirit is not to judge the temporal as bad. We are to care for the physical, tend to our environment, and honor the artwork of the master Artist. The Heavens have been made for God but the earth He has entrusted to mankind (Psalm 115:16).

However, for far too long we have only been aware of that which is seen (which is temporal) and ignored the Spirit (Who is eternal). This lesson clarifies our perspective and priorities, honoring the Spirit as teacher and helper to us while we live in these earthen vessels.

Enjoy and delight in this world of form, its seasons, its colors, its beauty, yet remain anchored in your identity in Him and He in you. The time has come for you to worship God, who is Spirit, in spirit and in Truth.

REFLECT ON THESE QUESTIONS

1. When you think of Heaven, how do you picture it?

_____

_____

2. Now picture the Kingdom of Heaven—the one that Jesus said isn't coming with signs because it's already in your midst (within you). Try to describe it.

_____

_____

3. When you see the Scripture that says that all things consist in Him and are held together by Him, how does that make you see yourself?

_____

_____

4. What would you say is your biggest challenge to "seeing" the Kingdom of Heaven which is now here?

_____

_____

SCRIPTURES AND REFLECTIONS FROM THE MEDITATION

1. *John 17:3* *This is eternal life, that they may know You, the only true God, and Jesus Christ whom You have sent.*

2. *1 Corinthians 13:12* *For now we see in a mirror dimly, but then face to face; now I know in part, but then I will know fully just as I also have been fully known.* *1 Corinthians 2:16* *"Who has known the mind of the Lord, that he will instruct him?" But we have the mind of Christ.* *1 John 2:20* *But you have an anointing from the Holy One, and you all know.*

Though we don't experience the spiritual dimension fully now, we know more about it than we understand. That is, we have intimate union with our Father, even as a child knows its mother without being taught everything about her. Like that child, we don't yet understand all that we know. But we can rest assured in this revelation, that God is infinitely good and complete.

3. *Luke 17:20-21* *Now having been questioned by the Pharisees as to when the kingdom of God was coming, He answered them and said, "The kingdom of God is not coming with signs to be observed; nor will they say, 'Look, here it is!' or, 'There it is!' For behold, the kingdom of God is in your midst."*

We look outside of ourselves for what we believe we don't possess. But everything we need in God is already within reach, as we will discover when we seek His kingdom above all else. All of our longings can be summed up as a longing for a relationship with God himself, in Christ through the power of the Holy Spirit.

4. *John 1:4-5 In Him was life, and the life was the Light of men. The Light shines in the darkness, and the darkness did not comprehend it.*

Light is not offended, worn out, or overpowered by darkness. As long as a light is shining, it doesn't even know the darkness exists. It can't, for the source of light sees nothing but what it illuminates. It doesn't have to fight against the darkness. It simply does what it was created to do. It shines.

5. **Colossians 1:17** *He is before all things, and in Him all things hold together.*

There is nothing that exists apart from Him, without His knowledge, or without His involvement. This doesn't mean that God is behind evil. In our blindness we abuse the creation we have been given to steward. To abuse means to use something for a purpose other than for which it was intended. A hammer was created to pound a nail. Have you ever hit your thumb with a hammer? When a creation forgets its purpose, brutal consequences can result. Wisdom recognizes purpose in creation and works with it to bring about the best possible outcome.

6. **Psalm 139:8** *Where can I go from Your Spirit? Or where can I flee from Your presence? If I ascend to heaven, You are there; If I make my bed in Sheol, behold, You are there.*

Is there anywhere that God is not present, if He is indeed omnipresent? The trees are not God, but He clearly exists in them because He is everywhere. If Christ, as the Light of the world, is interwoven even on a subatomic level with matter, why does He seem so distant? Because we have been led to believe that He is. Much modern church passion is tied to a desire to find God or be close to God. But the psalmist realized that God is not hard to find. You can't get away from the One who holds all things together.

7. *John 17:3 This is eternal life, that they may know You, the only true God, and Jesus Christ whom You have sent.*

When does eternal life begin? Because the entire concept of *eternal* transcends linear time, it is impossible for eternal life to have a beginning. You are a multidimensional being, able to be in both time (here in this world of form) and eternity (seated in heavenly places now) at the very same time. So your eternity has already begun by this very realization. In Him you live and move and have your being.

From our perspective, God appears to work with and within time, for it is the existence that we know. But the dimension of heaven may be to us as difficult to comprehend as the universe is to a baby. Consider that God's timelessness may perhaps be best seen in His ability to move freely throughout time to ultimately make all things work together for good for you. Whatever theories we come up with, God will always exceed our expectations, for God is better than we think, and we cannot imagine Him to be better than He is.

8. *2 Corinthians 4:17 We look not to the things that are seen, but to the things that are unseen. For the things that are seen are transient, but the things that are unseen are eternal.*

9. *Mark 12:30-31 "Love the Lord your God with all your heart, and with all your soul, and with all your mind, and with all your strength . . . You shall love your neighbor as yourself." There is no other commandment greater than these.*

Compare this with the following verse. *Luke 14:26 If anyone comes to Me, and does not hate his own father and mother and wife and children and brothers and sisters, yes, and even his own life, he cannot be My disciple.*

Followers of Jesus's Way are awakening to this reality. Our authentic identity, which we embrace, is "in Him." Our false identity is every label that we have been identified with that is other than "in Him." Jesus tells us to "hate" these roles (child, parent, spouse), which means we must hold them of no account in our search for identity.

As Paul wrote in *Galatians 3:28 There is neither Jew nor Greek, there is neither slave nor free man, there is neither male nor female; for you are all one in Christ Jesus.* Your nationality, your gender, and your cultural position are not who you truly are. Nor is your job title, your résumé, or your social status. When you surrender who you think you are to who you truly are—a child of your Father—then the divine nature of your Father (who is Love) will be the very Spirit that you put on display. This is how our fruits are known.

10. *2 Corinthians 4:16, 18 Therefore we do not lose heart, but though our outer man is decaying, yet our inner man is being renewed day by day*

. . . while we look not at the things which are seen, but at the things which are unseen; for the things which are seen are temporal, but the things which are not seen are eternal.

11. ***2 Corinthians 5:13*** NIV *If we are "out of our mind," as some say, it is for God; if we are in our right mind, it is for you.*

The bliss of union with God can cause joy to erupt from within you like a person who has fallen in love. Paul lets people know that he'll hold it together when he's around them, but otherwise he may seem out of his mind. What could cause such a joy that transcends human intelligence? The realization that you are one with God in Christ by the power of the Holy Spirit. And that your unity with Him is the result of His desire and design, not your worthiness. This is grace.

12. ***2 Corinthians 5:16*** ESV *From now on, therefore, we regard no one according to the flesh. Even though we once regarded Christ according to the flesh, we regard him thus no longer.*

It is impossible to know Jesus without realizing this truth. You are, at the eternal core of your being, spirit, not body.

John 4:24 *God is spirit and those who worship Him must worship in spirit and in truth.*

God is spirit and so are you. Your costume, beautiful as it may be, is temporal. We commune in this world of flesh and form, but don't mistake anyone's external costume, nor all of its labels, for the true person you see before you. See what your Father sees in others and in yourself.

13. ***Galatians 6:8*** *For the one who sows to his own flesh will from the flesh reap corruption, but the one who sows to the Spirit will from the Spirit reap eternal life.*

NINE
WHAT DEFIES EARTHLY EYES

All that is perishable are beautiful gifts…but only as you let go of them can you find true delight in them.

LETTING GO

After considering so deeply the idea of taking hold of the Kingdom within, it may seem ironic to begin to speak of letting go. But to know that Kingdom requires letting go of attachment to that which is temporal. True love, joy, and peace do not come from the temporal realm. They can be communicated and enjoyed in the temporal realm but they don't originate there. When you realize this, then nothing that happens to you in this realm can threaten the source of your love, joy, and peace.

After the resurrection, something interesting happens. Jesus appears bodily, but wasn't recognized by Mary Magdalene who thought He was just a gardener. Mark says He appeared to two others who knew him well on the road to Emmaus but it took them a long time to recognize Jesus, and then only when He opens their eyes to see. By the time He appears to the disciples, He has to show Thomas the scars in His hands, feet, and side for Thomas to know it's Him. Why? Surely Thomas would have recognized Jesus by His face alone. And speaking of face, wasn't Jesus's body brutalized before His death? Were all of His other wounds healed? What did He look like to Thomas and the disciples?

It appears that after the resurrection, Jesus' body had changed. By the time He appears to John in Revelation, though recognizable in form, His body clearly has some upgrades. The point is that the flesh, though a gift from God, is subject to the Spirit. The physical is subject to the Spiritual and the kingdom of this world is subject to His Kingdom which rules over all.

And is it not the same with you? Paul is clear, your body will pass away. Why, then, place your identity in that which is temporal? You are seamlessly integrated with your body, but it is temporary, lasting only a day longer or some years longer. In truth, it's already dying. Even what we call healing of the body, is only postponing the disease that eventually kills every body—death. Death has no sting when you realize that it's only your costume dying, not you.

Life on earth, in this body, will eventually end in that body's death. Thankfully, you yourself don't die. You are eternal. So let go of your earthly attachment to your physical life. Only then can you enjoy it for the short time you are in it.

REFLECT ON THESE QUESTIONS

1. Name five temporal roles you have played or currently play in this temporal world. Which roles bring you the most joy?

_____

_____

2. Who would you be without those roles?

_____

_____

3. If you had to let go of every physical role you play, which one would be the hardest to let go of and why?

_____

_____

4. There are many roles we play that don't serve us well. What roles are you attached to that work against your ability to see and abide in who you are as the son or daughter of God?

_____

_____

ACTIVATION

Gather together with another person or a few people and, together, do the following exercise. Describe yourself in as much detail as you can in under two minutes, but you are not allowed to speak of your past or your temporal life. Notice how difficult this is, because we are tied so strongly to defining ourselves on the basis of what we have or know as the story of our lives in body alone.

Now describe the other person to them from this same perspective. Tell them who they are, right now, in as much detail as you can. Ask the Father to show you what He sees and then tell them what you see and hear. Communicate the impressions in your heart that are marked by love and compassion as the Holy Spirit unveils the treasure of their identity to you.

SCRIPTURES AND REFLECTIONS FROM THE MEDITATION

1. *John 20:27* *Then He said to Thomas, "Reach here with your finger, and see My hands; and reach here your hand and put it into My side; and do not be unbelieving, but believing."*

2. *1 Corinthians 15:44* *It* (the body) *is sown a natural body, it is raised a spiritual body. If there is a natural body, there is also a spiritual body.*

    1 Corinthians 15:50 *Now I say this, brethren, that flesh and blood cannot inherit the kingdom of God; nor does the perishable inherit the imperishable.*

3. *John 17:11* *I am no longer in the world; and yet they themselves are in the world, and I come to You. Holy Father, keep them in Your name, the name which You have given Me, that they may be one even as We are.*

    Where is Jesus while He's praying this? Clearly He's standing on earth. But He said He's not in this world, and He spoke truth. How can this be? He was with them, but their perspective of this life didn't match His yet. Does ours?

John 17:15-16 I do not ask You to take them out of the world, but to keep them from the evil one. They are not of the world, even as I am not of the world.

In Him, you are here in form, but your authentic identity is in Him, seated in heavenly places. We are learning to reflect the light of heaven in the darkness of this world, for you are the light of the world.

4. *2 Corinthians 5:16-17 Therefore from now on we recognize no one according to the flesh . . . Therefore if anyone is in Christ, he is a new creature; the old things passed away; behold, new things have come.*

You are not a refurbished wreck. You are a creation that has never been seen before. An entirely new creature that has no other point of reference for being than the One in whose image and likeness you are created. With this in mind, you *must* see Him in order to know who you are.

5. *2 Corinthians 4:7 ESV But we have this treasure in jars of clay, to show that the surpassing power belongs to God and not to us.*

2 Corinthians 5:1 ESV For we know that if the tent that is our earthly home is destroyed, we have a building from God, a house not made with hands, eternal in the heavens.

After the resurrection, Jesus is recognized in physical form, even showing the scars of the crucifixion. But in his Revelation, John also sees Jesus, and though He is still recognizable in a body, this form is unlike anything John has ever seen before. He can barely describe the glory of it (Revelation 6:11-16). However we will be known in the realm of heaven, it won't be by this mortal flesh we now inhabit, which is subject to age, decay, injury, pain, and disease. Care for this costume you wear, for you are a dwelling place of the Spirit of God, but know that you won't be dragging this body and its issues into eternity. Your body is not you. Who you are is far more beautiful.

2 Corinthians 4:18 NIV So we fix our eyes (perception) *not on what is seen, but on what is unseen, since what is seen is temporary, but what is unseen is eternal.*

2 Corinthians 5:16 Therefore from now on we recognize no one according to the flesh; even though we have known Christ according to the flesh, yet now we know Him in this way no longer.

Do you ever think about your spirit? Do you know that you are a spiritual being? Try something today. Ignore everybody's costume and ask your Father to reveal to you how He sees the people you encounter. When it comes to a person's costume, refuse to be offended by anything temporal. Love them as God loves them. See that what you do to the least in your eyes, you do to Christ. If you don't know who a person really is, start here: everyone is a much-loved child of God, made in His image. Remember, that is who you are, too.

6. **Colossians 3:1-3 NIV** *Since then you have been raised with Christ, set your hearts on things above* (beyond)*, where Christ is, seated at the right hand of God. Set your minds on things above, not on earthly things. For you have died and life is now hidden with Christ in God.*

7. **Matthew 6:24** *No one can serve two masters; for either he will hate the one and love the other, or he will be devoted to one and despise the other. You cannot serve God and mammon.*

8. **Genesis 1:26 ESV** *Then God said, "Let us make man in our image, after our likeness. And let them have dominion over the fish of the sea and over the birds of the heavens and over the livestock and over all the earth and over every creeping thing that creeps on the earth."*

How do you define *dominion*? Is it "to rule, control, and dominate" or "to love, protect, and serve?" How did Jesus demonstrate the Father's nature here on earth? Whatever power, intelligence, and inventive brilliance we exercise here must have love as its foundation, or it's of no value.

Psalm 115:16 *The heavens are the heavens of the Lord, But the earth He has given to the sons of men.* The restoration of your authentic identity will open your eyes to care for this world that He entrusted to you. See the beauty of this world around you as a gift from your Father. Bless it and do not curse it, for you are restored in Him.

9. **Matthew 11:28-30** *Come to Me, all who are weary and heavy-laden, and I will give you rest. Take My yoke upon you and learn from Me, for I am gentle and humble in heart, and you will find rest for your souls. For My yoke is easy and My burden is light.*

As we've seen earlier, the *yoke* in rabbinical culture referred to the way that particular rabbi interpreted the Scriptures. The teachings of Jesus

THE FORGOTTEN WAY | STUDY GUIDE

are complex, but not complicated. Think of a beautiful diamond with many facets. A geologist can study the diamond for its complexity, and a bride can admire it for its worth and brilliance, but a child can hold the diamond and equally enjoy its beauty without a full understanding of its makeup or its value.

Psalm 62:1-2 My soul waits in silence for God only; From Him is my salvation. He only is my rock and my salvation, My stronghold; I shall not be greatly shaken.

10. *John 16:33 These things I have spoken to you, so that in Me you may have peace. In the world you have tribulation* (trouble), *but take courage; I have overcome the world.*

Have you spent your life trying to crucify your flesh, or are you living the joy of the resurrected life as a child of your victorious Father? It has been said that peace is not the absence of conflict, but the presence of Jesus. Every word Jesus said was to impart peace into you. If the words of Jesus frightened you or caused your heart any response other than peace, you have missed the point. Go back and ask Him to reveal His peace to you through His Spirit and His Word.

Romans 8:37 ESV No, in all these things we are more than conquerors through him who loved us.

How can you be *more* than a conqueror? It's like being the wife of a champion boxer; when the fight is over, he hands you the check. You didn't swing a single punch, but you reap the full benefits of a victory that someone else won. Or you can think of it like an inheritance, in which you receive a wealth that someone else worked for and passed on to you out of love. It's the inexplicable wonder of the love and grace of your Father. In this way Jesus died for your sin.

11. *Matthew 7:7 Ask, and it will be given to you; seek, and you will find; knock, and it will be opened to you.* Compare that verse to *James 4:3 You ask and do not receive, because you ask with wrong motives, so that you may spend it on your pleasures.* Then meditate on *Mark 11:24 Therefore I say to you, all things for which you pray and ask, believe that you have received them, and they will be granted you.*

The key here is the phrase "when you pray." To pray is to give your attention to the presence of God. What are the desires that arise in your heart when you're in His presence, fully aware of Him? Give attention to those.

1 John 5:14-15 *This is the confidence which we have before Him, that, if we ask anything according to His will, He hears us. And if we know that He hears us in whatever we ask, we know that we have the requests which we have asked from Him.*

TEN

SEEING IN THE DARK

If shame and deception can blind, Yeshua's love can bring sight to the blind. Through a renewing of the mind, empowered by the Spirit, one can see.

THE POWER OF THE RENEWED MIND

This meditation contains a powerful story of people who, because of extreme trauma to the mind, made a purposeful determination not to see. As much of a tragedy as it is to have working eyes that you refuse to use, it is an equal tragedy to be blind, yet claim to see.

Jesus taught much about blindness in both the physical and the Spiritual realm. He encountered people who were blind and He made their physical eyes see. In opening their eyes they also saw His heart and got a revelation of who He was. Healing is just one of the ways in which the Father's love was demonstrated. When He encountered religious leaders in John 9 who thought they could see, He revealed that they were, in fact, blind. In a remarkable observance, there is no record of physical blindness that He could not heal, but there were many religious people who persisted in the blindness. Though He challenged them constantly, He refused to violate their own will.

So much of Jesus' teaching is impossible to grasp unless we allow the Holy Spirit to shift our perception. Unless the Spirit brings life to what is written, that letter can kill. As Paul wrote in reference to Scripture: *For the letter kills but the Spirit gives life.* But as your mind is renewed by the presence of the indwelling Word, who is Jesus, your thoughts and words will reflect His life in you.

Let go of fear, let go of shame, let go of powerlessness and rest in the empowering grace of Jesus. Remember Jesus sleeping in the boat as the storm tosses it about and terrorizes the other passengers who are all too aware of only the wind, waves, and their own mortality. The peace within Him was greater than the storm around Him. If there's any picture of how the realm of Spirit is superior to the temporal realm, even in the face of opposing circumstances, it is this story. It would make more sense to calm the storm and then rest. But Jesus rests within the storm, and what a priceless lesson. You see, there is no circumstance that can shake that which is anchored in the Kingdom that is unshakable.

REFLECT ON THESE QUESTIONS

1. If you had a renewed mind, how would you see yourself right now?

_____

_____

2. Imagine for a moment and answer, how would a renewed mind filled with love, joy, and peace see the world and the people in it?

_____

_____

3. How is that different from how you have seen yourself and the world until now?

_____

_____

4. What are the most threatening waves on the sea of your life right now? Is there a way for you to see peace in the midst of that storm?

_____

_____

SCRIPTURES AND REFLECTIONS FROM THE MEDITATION

1. *John 3:1-3 Now there was a man of the Pharisees, named Nicodemus, a ruler of the Jews; this man came to Jesus by night and said to Him, "Rabbi, we know that You have come from God as a teacher; for no one can do these signs that You do unless God is with him." Jesus answered and said to him, "Truly, truly, I say to you, unless one is born again he cannot see the kingdom of God."*

Yeshua offers an answer to a question that hasn't even been asked yet. He reveals that your awakening in Him (the new birth) is what opens your eyes to see the kingdom of God.

2. *Matthew 6:22-23 The eye is the lamp of the body; so then if your eye is clear, your whole body will be full of light. But if your eye is bad, your whole body will be full of darkness. If then the light that is in you is darkness, how great is the darkness!*

Notice that Yeshua said 'eye' not 'eyes.' He wasn't talking about the eyes in your head, but your perception of reality. When attention is given to the fullness of light, that spiritual perspective has a dramatic effect on our experience in bodily form. Could it be that a key to healing can be found in how we see?

3. *Matthew 5:29 If your right eye makes you stumble, tear it out and throw it from you; for it is better for you to lose one of the parts of your body, than for your whole body to be thrown into hell.*

4. *Matthew 13:14 NIV You will be ever hearing but never understanding; you will be ever seeing but never perceiving.*

5. *1 John 1:5-10 God is Light, and in Him there is no darkness at all. If we say that we have fellowship with Him and yet walk in the darkness, we lie and do not practice the truth; but if we walk in the Light as He Himself is in the Light, we have fellowship with one another, and the blood of Jesus His Son cleanses us from all sin.*

If we say that we have no sin, we are deceiving ourselves and the truth is not in us.

Sin is missing the mark; all of that which separates us from the experience of our true identity as the sons and daughters of God. Do you have the capability to sin? Yes. In fact, most live in sin most of the time. But don't assume that your ability to miss the mark means that it is your truest nature to do so, because that nature who is you is risen with Christ. Missing the mark, however, is baked into your lower nature. Only in letting go of it, can you see your identity in Christ.

When we become aware of who we are, that is, when we walk in the light, then our minds are cleansed of all notions of separation in Christ and the lower nature is silenced.

You can choose sin, and as you do, you suffer its consequences in your life. But that sin doesn't change your identity. Letting go of false identities and surrendering to who we are *in Him* awakens us to the reality of our purity by His grace. That purity is a gift and is not partial. It's complete.

If, on the other hand, we say that we have no sin (anything that separates us from our intimate awareness of who we are) we are only being self-righteous because we all lose sight of who we are far too often. But, again, that doesn't change who we are. We are the sons and daughters of the Father in Christ..

6. *Matthew 8:26 He said to them, "Why are you afraid, you men of little faith?" Then He got up and rebuked the winds and the sea, and it became perfectly calm.*

Yeshua could rest within the storm because there was no storm within Him. There is no need for a storm within you. Let go of your fear as you hear your Father speak peace to the waves. Join Him in this declaration and say what He is saying. "Peace, be still." To say what the Father is saying is to exercise the faith of Christ.

When there is no storm in you, nothing will have the power to threaten you. Yeshua released the dimension of heaven from within Him to affect the world around Him.

ELEVEN

SEEING IS BELIEVING

*In Yeshua's light, all darkness flees. In His light, which
is now your own, all shame is replaced by honor, all
grievance is traded for forgiveness, all sorrow turned to
joy, all pain but a shadow to pass before the sun.*

THE ENLIGHTENED HEART

We have learned that Jesus is the light of the world, and now He declares that you are the light of the world as well. So then the challenge is not to strive to become something but to simply learn to be who we already are. This is how we shine. You have the Spirit within you, so then Love is the core of your being. You already have the essence of love infused within you as your light, which is His. You already have the Spirit of truth within you.

How do you hear and how do you begin to see? The first step is to realize that to the extent you are seeing darkness, your vision is distorted. As Jesus said, if your perception is clear, you will see and experience light; if your perception is not clear, that light will appear darkened.

Your journey is now primarily one of seeing truth and that truth will set you free. Be aware that the light always shines. Your inability to see it in any given situation is only because you have masked the face of the light with a veil that hides it from your sight. Just knowing that the light is there, as bright as always, brings great relief.

In this meditation, you read the story of the stick in the water. Like the water that distorted the image of the stick, the world of offense will distort your vision of yourself, making you look crooked when, in truth, you are straight in the eyes of your Father because you are complete. Believing in your Father's goodness and love will draw you to the light, which is a love that covers all sin and keeps no record of wrong, even as He asks you to do the same. Anything less will constitute a grievance which blocks the light from you. Remove that plank of offense—that veil that hides the light—and you will see the light.

You can see light or you can see darkness in any storm. Choose to see light, believing it is there, seen with correct vision in faith. This is what allowed Jesus to sleep through the storm in peace, and upon waking, chiding his disciples for their lack of faith. Why are you afraid, my friends? Why do you see darkness instead of peace?

See today, see now, that the light is always there. See that you have always been loved by your Father. See that this book in your hands is, in some small way, the appointed moment that your Father has destined that you are to know this. Maybe for the first time or maybe to be reassured again, but in whatever state you have come, you are to know this now. Your Father sees you as pure, holy, and blameless in Christ. See this instead of the storm and you will have found peace.

REFLECT ON THESE QUESTIONS

1. Realizing that we can see peace instead of grievance in any situation is a difficult thing for many to grasp because we are enslaved by the world and so feel like victims to it. Do you believe that in Christ, you have overcome the world with Him even as you have died and been raised with Him?

_____

_____

2. Is there anything about you, your past, or your current situation that you find yourself condemning right now? How does that grievance make you feel?

_____

_____

3. How would you feel if you were able to let go of that offense against yourself or situation?

_____

_____

SCRIPTURES AND REFLECTIONS FROM THE MEDITATION

1. *Matthew 6:25, 31* Do not be worried about your life, as to what you will eat or what you will drink; nor for your body, as to what you will put on. Is not life more than food, and the body more than clothing? Do not worry then, saying, "What will we eat?" or "What will we drink?" or "What will we wear for clothing?"

2. *Matthew 25:24-30* And the one also who had received the one talent came up and said, "Master, I knew you to be a hard man, reaping where you did not sow and gathering where you scattered no seed. And I was afraid, and went away and hid your talent in the ground. See, you have what is yours." But his master answered and said to him, "You wicked, lazy slave, you knew that I reap where I did not sow and gather where I scattered no seed. Then you ought to have put my money in the bank, and on my arrival I would have received my money back with interest. Therefore take away the talent from him, and give it to the one who has the ten talents." For to everyone who has, more shall be given, and he will have an abundance; but from the one who does not have, even what he does have shall be taken away. Throw out the worthless slave into the outer darkness; in that place there will be weeping and gnashing of teeth.

Here we find a parable on the reality of reaping what you sow and the harsh system of the world. The harsh taskmaster is life, not God, and to cringe in fear at your lot in life and not use what is given you like this servant did, is only to suffer deeply in this life, cast out in utter darkness.

Instead, live life full of light and be bold with what is given you.

3. *John 16:33* These things I have spoken to you, so that in Me you may have peace. In the world you have tribulation, but take courage; I have overcome the world.

When you hear the authentic gospel, when the Word speaks, your soul is empowered to respond with courage and reflect the peace of heaven. Peace is the fruit of the Gospel.

4. *Luke 6:42* NIV How can you say to your brother, "Brother, let me take the speck out of your eye," when you yourself fail to see the plank in your

own eye? You hypocrite, first take the plank out of your eye, and then you will see clearly to remove the speck from your brother's eye.

In the context of love and humility, correcting our brothers and sisters is beautiful, because it unites and empowers rather than divides and controls.

5. *Genesis 3:9-13 Then the Lord God called to the man, and said to him, "Where are you?" He said, "I heard the sound of You in the garden, and I was afraid because I was naked; so I hid myself." And He said, "Who told you that you were naked? Have you eaten from the tree of which I commanded you not to eat?"*

This is one of the rare moments when God asks a question. He doesn't do this because He doesn't know where Adam is, but to expose that the man was now living in a self-generated perspective of separation from God.

The man said, "The woman whom You gave to be with me, she gave me from the tree, and I ate." Then the Lord God said to the woman, "What is this you have done?" And the woman said, "The serpent deceived me, and I ate."

Judgment is the fruit of the fall, and with it, guilt and shame.

6. *Matthew 5:14-16 You are the light of the world. A town built on a hill cannot be hidden. Neither do people light a lamp and put it under a bowl. Instead they put it on its stand, and it gives light to everyone in the house. In the same way, let your light shine before others, that they may see your good deeds and glorify your Father in heaven.*

7. *John 5:22, 45 NIV The Father judges no one . . . Neither will I accuse you before the Father. Your accuser is Moses* (the law) *in whom your hopes are set.*

8. *Luke 6:37 ESV Judge not, and you will not be judged.*

Why? Because your judgment is what judges you. The law of judgment (Moses) which is the natural system of the world, is what judges you, not your Father or Jesus.

9. *Hebrews 8:13 ESV In speaking of a new covenant, he makes the first one obsolete. And what is becoming obsolete and growing old is ready to vanish away.*

10. ***John 8:12*** Then Jesus again spoke to them, saying, "I am the Light of the world; he who follows Me will not walk in the darkness, but will have the Light of life."

11. ***Ephesians 1:17-22*** *That the God of our Lord Jesus Christ, the Father of glory, may give to you a spirit of wisdom and of revelation in the knowledge of Him.*

Authentic wisdom is a revelation of Jesus Christ.

I pray that the eyes of your heart may be enlightened, so that you will know what is the hope of His calling, what are the riches of the glory of His inheritance in the saints, and what is the surpassing greatness of His power toward us who believe. These are in accordance with the working of the strength of His might which He brought about in Christ, when He raised Him from the dead and seated Him at His right hand in the heavenly places, far above all rule and authority and power and dominion, and every name that is named, not only in this age but also in the one to come.

The implications of this are amazing beyond words. The cross did far more than deal with the sin and eternity issue. Yeshua restored you to your original design, beyond even what Adam experienced in the garden. You are indeed a new creation, one that has not been before.

And He put all things in subjection under His feet, and gave Him as head over all things to the church, which is His body, the fullness of Him who fills all in all.

You are created to be the mansion that God has chosen to fill with His presence.

You have come to the end of the Meditations 8 through 11 on the *Way* of Jesus which is, first, to *see* who you are in the eternal realm of the Father's presence now at hand.

Read and consider the third declaration

THE WAY

THE THIRD DECLARATION
Meditations 8-11

Your journey now is to see who you truly are, for you are the light of the world, the son or the daughter of your Father, a new creature flowing with more beauty and power than you have dared imagine possible.

TWELVE
SEE LIKE A CHILD
AND BE FREE

IWhen you know only a drop of the Father, your heart is as full as the ocean. When you only see a glimmer of His light, your eyes are like the sun. When you know only the tiniest seed of Yeshua, you blossom in the Tree of Life.

GROWING YOUNG

To know the Father is to be in intimate communion with the heart of God. In the Kingdom of Jesus, maturity looks like childlikeness. This isn't childishness—there's a distinct difference between being childlike and childish. To be childlike means to be trusting of the Father. You don't think to second guess your Father's goodness, or wonder if He loves you. No more doubting if you are forgiven, and no longer questioning if you are accepted. Childlikeness is resting in the love and grace of your Father. It isn't being simpleminded. It's surrendering to what He says about you.

When Jesus delighted in the revelation that's hidden from the intelligent and revealed to infants, He wasn't saying that intelligence is bad. He was revealing that a proud perspective of personal intellect will blind you from what you still need to know. A characteristic of the childlike heart is that you are willing to be taught something new and let go of something old, because learning a new revelation almost always requires unlearning an old one.

In so doing, you are surrendering your attachment to an old identity in exchange for awakening to your identity in Christ, you in Him and He in you. Exercising that faith, you will know the Father and His infinite goodness.

Pride in our own intelligence, on the other hand, blinds us to truth. Just like the disciples saw the waves and panicked as Jesus slept, our old nature sees trouble and scrambles to protect itself, thereby unwittingly joining with the darkness in the storm. But Jesus is at peace. Oh you of little faith—trust in the Father like a child and be free.

To believe is to see, and to see is to believe. Both come through surrender, but whichever comes first, one leads to the other. To surrender is to let go. Let go of all that you think you know so that you might truly know Him in Spirit and in Truth.

REFLECT ON THESE QUESTIONS

1. Think back to the last time you were caught up in a moment of worship. There, the things of this world grew strangely dim. In that moment, did you feel threatened by your circumstances or did you feel free?

_____

_____

2. What does it mean to you to be like a child?

_____

_____

3. Think of a time when you know that God was calling you out of the boat to step on the water despite all of the circumstances that seemed to be threatening you. What happened?

_____

_____

ACTIVATION

Enter a time of worship with music. If you can, listen to "Come to Me" by Bethel Music. Hear the call of Jesus, beckoning you from your troubles, because He is all you need. Take your eyes off the troubled seas around you and keep them on Jesus, who has overcome the world. Notice when your spirit lifts and the world falls strangely dim. In this, you are awakening to the Kingdom of Heaven at hand. Linger and be glad; your salvation has come.

SCRIPTURES AND REFLECTIONS FROM THE MEDITATION

1. *Matthew 11:25 At that time Jesus said, "I praise You, Father, Lord of heaven and earth, that You have hidden these things from the wise and intelligent and have revealed them to infants."*

Because the letter kills and the Spirit gives life, anyone surrendered to the Holy Spirit can know the Word. It is not a function of intellect. If our study of the letter alone were the key to "knowing" God, we would not have killed Him when He came in the flesh.

2. *Matthew 18:3 NIV Truly I tell you, unless you change and become like little children, you will never enter the kingdom of heaven.*

The childlike heart is vulnerable, teachable, joyful, creative, and filled with wonder. There's a difference between being childish and childlike. Childishness is a posture of stubborn challenge. Childlikeness is a perspective of hopeful curiosity. Every question you ever ask is one of either challenge or curiosity. Let childlike wonder awaken in you again as you let go of all offense at the past and fear of the future.

3. *John 14:8-10 Philip said to Him, "Lord, show us the Father, and it is enough for us." Jesus said to him, "Have I been so long with you, and yet you have not come to know Me, Philip? He who has seen Me has seen the Father; how can you say, 'Show us the Father?' Do you not believe that I am in the Father, and the Father is in Me?"*

4. *Matthew 6:10 Your kingdom come. Your will be done, On earth as it is in heaven.*

Jesus reveals the will of the Father so this world can reflect His world. He desires that this dimension will bear the image of that dimension in every way. When you desire the same thing, you invite the Father to reveal to you the dimension in the Holy Spirit filled with love, joy, and peace. The first step into seeing that world is to simply accept that there is no distance between you and your Father right now. Yes, right now.

5. *Luke 14:28 ESV For which of you, desiring to build a tower, does not first sit down and count the cost, whether he has enough to complete it?*

Jesus makes the point that every investment requires sacrifice. Count the cost and compare it to the reward. In the case of choosing to follow Yeshua's Way, the joy of the return makes the sacrifice of letting go insignificant, though it might not seem so at the time. Letting go always requires faith, but after a while, letting go becomes natural. But just because you've mastered the art of letting go doesn't mean you have to be okay with loss. Some losses hurt deeply, yet the joy to come is priceless.

6. *Matthew 16:26 For what will it profit a man if he gains the whole world and forfeits his soul?*

7. *Matthew 13:44-46 The kingdom of heaven is like a treasure hidden in the field, which a man found and hid again; and from joy over it he goes and sells all that he has and buys that field. Again, the kingdom of heaven is like a merchant seeking fine pearls, and upon finding one pearl of great value, he went and sold all that he had and bought it.*

The kingdom of heaven is the realm of the King's domain, and that kingdom is always within reach. The realm of the kingdom is priceless beyond description and closer than you can imagine.

8. *Romans 12:2 Do not be conformed to this world, but be transformed by the renewing of your mind, so that you may prove what the will of God is, that which is good and acceptable and perfect.*

Learning a new revelation almost always requires that you unlearn an old one. To love learning is to also embrace the process of unlearning. The world is full of common sense, because, well, it's common. But a renewed mind sees beyond what is common sense.

9. *Ephesians 1:18 I pray that the eyes of your heart may be enlightened, so that you will know what is the hope of His calling, what are the riches of the glory of His inheritance in the saints.*

Hope is the joyful expectancy of good. There is a difference between expectation and expectancy. Expectation creates a box that must be filled with a certain thing a certain way in order for us to be happy. Expectancy has no boxes. It simply assumes that good is coming and is happy about it before it even shows up. The eyes of your heart are enlightened when you're filled with joy at the thought of your Father's voice before you've even heard it.

10. *Ephesians 2:8 For by grace you have been saved through faith; and that not of yourselves, it is the gift of God.*

11. ***Proverbs 3:5-6*** NIV *Trust in the Lord with all your heart and lean not on your own understanding; in all your ways submit to him, and he will make your paths straight.*

There is no rest apart from trust, and trust is appropriately placed only in Him. Pay attention to the reality of His presence in all your ways. We are lost and our ways go wrong when we perceive God as distant and separate from us.

12. ***Matthew 8:24-26*** *And behold, there arose a great storm on the sea, so that the boat was being covered with the waves; but Jesus Himself was asleep. And they came to Him and woke Him, saying, "Save us, Lord; we are perishing!" He said to them, "Why are you afraid, you men of little faith?" Then He got up and rebuked the winds and the sea, and it became perfectly calm.* ***Matthew 14:25*** *And in the fourth watch of the night He came to them, walking on the sea.*

13. ***Matthew 11:28-30*** *Come to Me, all who are weary and heavy-laden, and I will give you rest. Take My yoke upon you and learn from Me, for I am gentle and humble in heart, and you will find rest for your souls. For My yoke is easy and My burden is light.*

THIRTEEN
BEAUTIFUL, BEAUTIFUL BROTHER AND SAVIOR

*Purification is removing all that keeps you blind to the
staggering reality that Yeshua has taken
you into His heart.*

SURRENDER TO SIGHT

You've known the love of Jesus. Many have. You've heard now how the Father loves you. Fewer have known this. You've now heard of the mysterious union between you and Jesus, as explained by both Paul and Jesus. Even fewer have known this. You may now be wondering, "How can I make these revelations a reality? How do I live this? How can I understand this mystery? How can I see the unseen?" There is no striving to see.

There is only surrendering that which blocks your vision.

There is no fear in love because fear has to do with punishment, He only corrects that which distorts your vision and for this, you need not fear Him, but thank Him. Remember, you cannot love what you fear.

We are in awe at the Father's goodness, and trembling in awe, we draw near, surrendering to the embrace of Love Himself. Now love is no longer a concept or an idea, but an experience.

Jesus demonstrated a life of surrender. Have you ever thought of Jesus as struggling? He struggled in the desert. He was deeply challenged in the garden. According to Hebrews 5 He submitted to the process of experience in flesh and learned obedience. So then, He had no advantage over you.

In fact, it could be said that you have an advantage because Jesus, once He became perfected according to Hebrews 5, became the way for you, as you align yourself with Him. How? He died for your sin. He died so that you could become one with Him, seated in the Heavenly places even now. Your awareness of your identity in Christ grows as you surrender yourself to this truth. And as your awareness of your true identity blossoms, you are saved from suffering in the storms of this life and in the life to come.

It is said, pain is inevitable, but suffering is optional. You might not escape the waves, but you can find peace in them. Pain will come, ending in death, but you can be saved from the suffering that this short life offers you.

Jesus suffered and learned obedience in that suffering. But you don't have to suffer. All you have to do is place your faith in Him and in your union with Him, having already died with Him, and risen with Him.

Your journey now is simply to surrender everything in this world that you've placed your security in, for who you are in Christ.

REFLECT ON THESE QUESTIONS

1. What does it mean to you to surrender all you think you know, to be who you truly are?

_____

_____

2. Describe a time in your life when you experienced pain and yet found yourself transcending that storm to find peace.

_____

_____

3. As you meditate on the thought that Jesus learned obedience through all that He suffered as recorded in Hebrews 5, what new thoughts come to you? Does it draw you to Him or away from Him?

_____

_____

SCRIPTURES AND REFLECTIONS FROM THE MEDITATION

1. *John 14:23-24 Jesus answered and said to him, "If anyone loves Me, he will keep My word; and My Father will love him, and We will come to him and make Our abode with him. He who does not love Me does not keep My words."*

Obedience is simply alignment. It is to surrender to union with God in Christ by the power of the Holy Spirit. Obedience is not about rules, but about the relationship of love found in the presence of your Father. Look at Paul's letters of instruction to the churches. He never itemizes all the commands of Jesus, emphasizing obedience to those. Instead he capitalizes upon this revelation of union with Christ and then addresses specific issues a church is dealing with. Paul knows that unless we get a revelation of how much we are in Christ, we'll just become religious.

But once we awaken to that reality of being in Him, the secure love of our father will become our life source. We will then love as He loves us, and love is the sum of all Jesus's commandments: love God by aligning with Him in the vine, and love our neighbors as ourselves.

2. *Mark 10:6-8 From the beginning of creation, God made them male and female. "For this reason a man shall leave his father and mother, and the two shall become one flesh"; so they are no longer two, but one flesh. What therefore God has joined together, let no man separate.*

This is Jesus speaking about marriage and divorce. Keep this in mind when you read the next verse, written by Paul.

Ephesians 5:30-32 We are members of His body. "For this reason a man shall leave his father and mother, and the two shall become one flesh." This mystery is great; but I am speaking with reference to Christ and the church.

Paul interprets the Genesis passage through the lens of union with Christ. Paul understands that the union of marriage here on earth is only a shadow of the reality of loving union that we have with God in Christ.

3. *Matthew 5:8 Blessed are the pure in heart, for they shall see God.*

The pure heart is made manifest by gratitude for the grace that accomplished what you could have never done on your own. The only way a heart can be pure is if the One who is holy steps into it.

4. *Galatians 3:26-28 You are all sons of God through faith in Christ Jesus. For all of you who were baptized into Christ have clothed yourselves with Christ. There is neither Jew nor Greek, there is neither slave nor free man, there is neither male nor female; for you are all one in Christ Jesus.*

It is baptism that "clothes" you in Christ. Is baptism to mean more than we may have thought?

Matthew 28:19 Go therefore and make disciples of all the nations, baptizing them in the name of the Father and the Son and the Holy Spirit,

This is not simply a scripted line to be recited over someone as the minister plunges them under the water. To baptize is to immerse or saturate. In Hebrew culture, someone's name is equivalent to his identity. So the revelation meant to be imparted in water baptism may be better understood if it said, "Be immersed in the identity of Father, Son, and Holy Spirit." Baptism is a physical reflection of a spiritual reality, namely, that you are clothed and complete in Him.

The objective isn't to give anyone a new label such as "Christian" as much as to make them disciples of the way of Yeshua, a way we too often forget each day.

5. *Luke 6:35 But love your enemies, and do good, and lend, expecting nothing in return; and your reward will be great, and you will be sons of the Most High; for He Himself is kind to ungrateful and evil men.*

6. *James 1:2-4 Consider it all joy, my brethren, when you encounter various trials, knowing that the testing of your faith produces endurance. And let endurance have its perfect result, so that you may be perfect and complete, lacking in nothing.*

7. *Romans 8:29 NIV For those God foreknew He also predestined to be conformed to the image of His Son, that He might be firstborn among many brothers and sisters. Hebrews 2:10-11 NIV In bringing many sons and daughters to glory, it was fitting that God, for whom and through whom everything exists, should make the pioneer of their salvation (Jesus) perfect through what He suffered. Both the one (Jesus) who makes people holy,*

and those who are made holy (you) *are of the same family. So Jesus is not ashamed to call them brothers and sisters.*

What do you usually get from your older brother when you're a kid? Well, usually you get hand-me-down clothes. Read *John 17:22* and find out how much more you get from Jesus: *The glory which You have given Me I have given to them, that they may be one, just as We are one.*

8. *Hebrews 4:15* NIV *For we do not have a high priest* (Jesus)*who is unable to empathize with our weaknesses, but we have one who has been tempted in every way, just as we are, yet he did not sin.*

He was tempted just as we are, and the way we are tempted in this life is over and over again, every day—that's what makes it difficult. His temptation wasn't a one-time affair, but was just as continual as our own, all the way to His death.

9. *Matthew 4:1-2* *Then Jesus was led up by the Spirit into the wilderness to be tempted by the devil. And after He had fasted forty days and forty nights, He then became hungry.*

10. *Mark 14:33-35* *And He took with Him Peter and James and John, and began to be very distressed and troubled. And He said to them, "My soul is deeply grieved to the point of death; remain here and keep watch." And He went a little beyond them, and fell to the ground and began to pray that if it were possible, the hour might pass Him by.*

11. *Hebrews 5:7-9* NIV *During the days of Jesus' life on earth, He offered up prayers and petitions with fervent cries and tears to the one who could save Him from death, and He was heard because of His reverent submission. Son though He was, He learned obedience from what He suffered and, once made perfect, He became the source of eternal salvation for all who obey Him.*

To truly obey means to align yourself with someone, not just in deed but in thought and nature. Jesus said in *John 12:49* *For I did not speak on My own initiative, but the Father Himself who sent Me has given Me a commandment as to what to say and what to speak.*

He is demonstrating a lifestyle of relationship with the Father. He is showing us what it is like to live in union with God by the power of the Holy Spirit.

12. *1 Corinthians 15:45* *So also it is written, "The first man, Adam, became a living soul." The last Adam became a life-giving spirit.*

Jesus does exactly the opposite of the first Adam, and Paul makes clear that Jesus is the last Adam. There is not another.

13. *Luke 22:42* *Father, if You are willing, remove this cup from Me; yet not My will, but Yours be done.*

In the garden of Eden, Adam chooses his own will over God's and eats of the tree of the knowledge of good and evil. In that act, man said to God, "Not thy will, but my will be done." Yeshua, the last Adam, in the second garden, sweats blood from a brow that will be pierced with a crown of thorns and thistles, and through the sweat and blood He says to the Father, "Not My will, but Thy will be done." And so reverses the first Adam's choice.

FOURTEEN
STEP OUT OF YOUR PRISON

*All of your life comes down to a very simple choice in
every moment What do you choose to see?
Who will you put your faith in?*

UNITING THE DIVIDED MIND

There is an eternal contest where truth and lies compete for the attention of our perspective. We direct the energy and passion of our lives to manifest the reality that we believe to be true. Empowered in the image and likeness of our Creator, we demonstrate that creative, Divine nature in more ways than can be described.

On the other hand, we are debilitated by the illusion of lies, and the affect of believing these lies is as powerful as our belief in the truth.

The lie says this is all there is. Your success will make you happy. Your money will put you at peace. Your job is your security. You will find yourself in your relationships. And yet, with the increase of material wealth, influence, and prestige comes increased pride and responsibility. In this world, to whom much is given, much is required. For every up, there is a down. And eye is required for an eye. This is the system of the world; the law of Moses, built upon the ego-based nature and the knowledge of good and evil.

Let go of the ego. Let go of the lie that you have no need of your Father. Place your identity in Jesus and let your heart fill with gratitude that your Father has formed you by His desire from a place of deep love. Surrender unites the divided mind because it lets go of the old nature and places your identity in His. It is surrender to all of Him being all of you. He doesn't erase you, He fulfills you. When you let go of your need to fulfill yourself, you are free to take joy in the indwelling presence of the Spirit and the eternal embrace of the Father.

There is only one relationship that completes you: Your relationship in Christ.

There are two worlds: The world of mammon and form, filled with both pleasure and suffering, rest and much striving, truth and many lies. And the Kingdom of your Father, filled with light without darkness, pleasure without suffering, peace without strife, and truth without lies.

Place your identity in one or the other. You cannot serve two masters.

REFLECT ON THESE QUESTIONS

1. In this world, do you feel more enslaved or free? Explain.

_____

_____

2. A divided mind lives in confusion and misery. Make a short list of those things that most frequently divide your mind.

_____

_____

3. What would your life be like if you abided in the vine, never being tossed like a wave on a sea of confusion and hard choices? Do you think this is possible for you in this life?

_____

_____

SCRIPTURES AND REFLECTIONS FROM THE MEDITATION

1. *Ephesians 2:4-9 But God, being rich in mercy, because of His great love with which He loved us, even when we were dead in our transgressions, made us alive together with Christ (by grace you have been saved), and raised us up with Him, and seated us with Him in the heavenly places in Christ Jesus, so that in the ages to come He might show the surpassing riches of His grace in kindness toward us in Christ Jesus. For by grace you have been saved through faith; and that not of yourselves, it is the gift of God; not as a result of works, so that no one may boast.*

If you died and rose and are now seated in heavenly places, you ascended with Christ. You are a multidimensional being, able to be in both time (here in this world of form) and eternity (seated in heavenly places now). You are a divinely created convergence of heaven and earth, made with a will to love so that you can fully participate in a relationship with your Father, who both made you and inhabits you in and through the Spirit. So your eternity has already begun. In Him you live and move and have your being. Now.

Colossians 3:1-4 NIV *Since, then, you have been raised with Christ, set your hearts on things above, where Christ is, seated at the right hand of God. Set your minds on things above, not on earthly things. For you died, and your life is now hidden with Christ in God. When Christ, who is your life, appears, then you also will appear with him in glory.*

We are made to observe, learn, and reflect, and whatever we behold, we become like. So we set our affection and attention on things above. The word *when* in the above verse is a progressive state of being (such as *whenever*) rather than a singular calendar event. So the verse is understood like this. Whenever Christ appears, you appear. Whenever Jesus is revealed, so are you.

2. *John 17:22* *The glory which You have given Me I have given to them.*

It is being in Christ that gives you access to His glory. Nothing of God originated with us or is carried by us independent of His presence. What a beautiful gift the Father has given us in Christ.

3. *Hebrews 4:2* *For indeed we have had good news preached to us, just as they also; but the word they heard did not profit them, because it was not united by faith in those who heard.*

God's belief is for you and not against you. But unbelief easily blinds Christians to the good news of who they are. When you believe a lie, you empower it to take a foothold in your mind, will, and emotions. A lie is a dis-ease to your soul, as powerful in its affect on your experience of life as is the truth. An encounter with God empowers you with the faith of Christ and puts your soul at rest.

4. *Matthew 19:24* *Again I say to you, it is easier for a camel to go through the eye of a needle, than for a rich man to enter the kingdom of*

God. It is not wealth or status or all this world has to offer that is evil, as is often quoted. Rather it is the *love* of wealth that is the root of all evil (1 Timothy 6:10). What we love reveals who we believe we are, because the affection of our hearts defines our identity in this world.

5. *Luke 14:26 If anyone comes to Me, and does not hate his own father and mother and wife and children and brothers and sisters, yes, and even his own life, he cannot be My disciple.*

6. *Luke 9:23 If anyone wishes come after Me, he must deny himself, and take up his cross daily and follow Me.*

Matthew 16:25 For whoever wishes to save his life will lose it; but whoever loses his life for My sake will find it.

You will never seek and find yourself outside of a revelation of Yeshua—only in Him can you be found. To see Him is to come to know who you truly are.

7. *Romans 14:23 Whatever is not from faith is sin.*

Consider that sin is whatever creates a perspective of distance between you and God. Faith is the pure river of life flowing from the oasis of our united relationship with Christ.

8. *1 Corinthians 6:12 All things are lawful for me, but not all things are profitable. All things are lawful for me, but I will not be mastered by anything.*

Just because all things are lawful for you, like Paul, doesn't mean that all serves you. Anything that blinds you to your identity in Christ, is missing the mark or sin, and that thing may be different for you than for your brother. That blindness (sin) doesn't change who you are, but it changes your experience of life and necessarily leads to misery. So seek to be mastered by nothing except Christ in you and you will experience true freedom.

9. *James 1:14 But each one is tempted when he is carried away and enticed by his own lust.*

It has been said that the same sun that melts ice, hardens clay. What carries you away? What blinds you? Whatever creates a sense of a barrier between you and God will blind you to who you truly are.

10. *Galatians 6:8 For the one who sows to his own flesh will from the flesh reap corruption, but the one who sows to the Spirit will from the Spirit reap eternal life.*

11. *1 Corinthians 13:12 For now we see in a mirror dimly, but then face to face; now I know in part, but then I will know fully just as I also have been fully known.*

THE WAY: SUMMARY

In the second section we have entered seven meditations on the *Way* of Yeshua, which is to *see* who you are in the eternal realm of the Father's presence now at hand by surrendering attachment to
all other identities.

These constitute the third and fourth declarations of The Forgotten Way.

THE THIRD DECLARATION
Meditations 8-11

Your journey now is to see who you truly are, *for you are the light of the world, the son or the daughter of your Father, a new creature flowing with more beauty and power than you have dared imagine possible.*

THE FOURTH DECLARATION
Meditations 12-14

You will only see who you are and thus be who you are as you surrender your attachment to all other identities, *which are like gods of a lesser power that block your vision of your true identity and keep you in darkness.*

III

THE LIFE

Yeshua made it plain: *I am the Way, the Truth and the Life.*

In this final section we will enter seven meditations (15-21) on our *Life* in Yeshua. This is the manifestation of the Father and ourselves on earth as we are in heaven, evidenced by love, joy, peace and power. And the greatest of these is love.

This constitutes the fifth declaration of The Forgotten Way.

THE FIFTH DECLARATION

Love, joy, and peace are the manifestation of your true identity *and the Father's realm, on earth as in heaven, through the power of the Holy Spirit.*

FIFTEEN
THE EVIDENCE OF YOU
IS LOVE

*You may look at your life and think He doesn't trust you,
but He sees you in His likeness and trusts you to the ends
of the earth. So trust Him.*

WITHOUT LOVE, ALL IS NOTHING

Much of the modern Christian quest has been misdirected. We long to escape earth, like the ancient gnostics, and go to heaven. But Jesus empowered us to bring heaven to earth. Or we place heaven on a shelf during this life, and seek to find our salvation from the storms of this life through all manner of pursuits and judgments that seem to give us significance and identity.

In either case, our quest is often misguided. Our true purpose is simple: To be who we are as the sons and daughters of the Father, and to manifest His love and will on earth as it is in Heaven.

We long to walk in power to heal, to prophesy, and have such faith that we could move mountains—all good things that require the power of God. But even so, they are nothing without love.

What kind of love? The kind of love that is kind to those who abuse us, as Jesus said. Anyone can love those who love them in return—truly that kind of love is maybe better described as addictive clinging.

True love, on the other hand, is supernatural, shown only by the sons and daughters of God who see no threat in the storms of this life.

But how can we love with this kind of love? Only by first seeing how we are loved. Through a revelation of the Father's love, you will find the extraordinary power to love as He loves. Our problem is that many *are* loving the way they think the Father loves—with a baseball bat and threats of punishment. How can we love others the way Jesus and Paul taught us to if we think the Father loves us in a much harsher way?

Remember that the very nature of God *is* Love. So then, Paul's love chapter (1 Corinthians 13) is a description of your Father. Now read it with new eyes and see that your Father *always trusts, always hopes, shows no arrogance, keeps no record of wrong, and is not provoked.*

Since you are made in His image and likeness, this is also a description of the authentic you. These traits of patience, kindness, keeping no record of wrongs, not being jealous, not easily provoked, rejoicing in truth, filled with belief, hope, endurance; none of these things inhibit individual expression. To see these traits emerge does not make us all look the same. Rather it empowers each of us to become a source of life for one another.

It is as Jesus taught in John 17:23. When we awaken to who we are in union with Him, then the world will know that the Father loves them in the same way He loves Jesus. Why? Because they will see the love in us, knowing by the evidence of love that we are His disciples. The evidence of your identity in Christ is love, so love even as He loves you. Love your Father. Love yourself. Love your neighbor as yourself.

REFLECT ON THESE QUESTIONS

1. When you travel the world or hang out with people who aren't Christians, do you see them as less loving and judgmental than the average Christian, or are they about the same? Why do you think most people (including Christians) openly describe Christians as sometimes being the most judgmental segment of our society?

_____

_____

2. Have you ever considered Paul's teaching that true love or the lack thereof is ultimately the only definitive quality in anyone's life? Does this ring true for you, or does it bring up resistance?

_____

_____

3. How well do you think you love, as Paul defines love? Can you imagine holding no record of wrong as your primary way of being in the world? What would it be like?

_____

_____

SCRIPTURES AND REFLECTIONS FROM THE MEDITATION

1. *1 Corinthians 13:12* *For now we see in a mirror dimly, but then face to face; now I know in part, but then I will know fully just as I also have been fully known.*

Is there any time when God has not known you? Is there any time when God forgot why He made you? Do you think you have disappointed your Father? You haven't. How can you disappoint someone who knows everything and loves you still? God doesn't manipulate you with His love. His love is an invitation for you to see what He has always seen in you and to know what He has always known about you: that you are both forgiven and innocent.

2. *Romans 14:17* *The kingdom of God is not eating and drinking, but righteousness and peace and joy in the Holy Spirit.* *Galatians 5:22-23* *The fruit of the Spirit is love, joy, peace, patience, kindness, goodness, faithfulness, gentleness, self-control; against such things there is no law.*

John 13:35 *By this all men will know that you are My disciples, if you have love for one another.*

3. *Mark 12:28-31* *One of the scribes came and heard them arguing, and recognizing that He had answered them well, asked Him, "What commandment is the foremost of all?" Jesus answered, "The foremost is, 'Hear, O Israel: The Lord our God, the Lord is one. And you shall love the Lord your God with all your heart and with all your soul and with all your*

mind and with all your strength.' The second is this: 'You shall love your neighbor as yourself.' There is no other commandment greater than these."

The core of love is often contrasted with wrath and judgment, as if these are equal and necessary opposing forces. But the Scriptures give love uncompromising importance. They never declare that God is wrath, but it is written that God *is* love. Wrath and mercy are not equal weights that create a healthy balance. All of what we think of as wrath is only purifying that which inhibits love in our lives. As such, it is healing, like an antibiotic that kills disease. When dis-ease is gone, ease and rest come.

4. *John 13:35 By this all men will know that you are My disciples, if you have love for one another.*

Mankind is blinded by division. Our awareness of our union with God in Christ by the power of the Holy Spirit will awaken the world.

5. *1 Corinthians 13:1-3 If I speak with the tongues of men and of angels, but do not have love, I have become a noisy gong or a clanging cymbal. If I have the gift of prophecy, and know all mysteries and all knowledge; and if I have all faith, so as to remove mountains, but do not have love, I am nothing. And if I give all my possessions to feed the poor, and if I surrender my body to be burned, but do not have love, it profits me nothing.*

It's possible to exercise spiritual gifts, perform supernatural miracles, have enviable intellect, and accomplish great works of social service that don't require God's involvement. But the only thing that gives us, or any work that we do, value, is the pure love of God. If you haven't figured this out by now, love is a big deal in the Bible. Without love, we and our works are nothing.

6. *John 14:16, 17, 20; 17:23 I will ask the Father, and He will give you another Helper, that He may be with you forever; that is the Spirit of truth, whom the world cannot receive, because it does not see Him or know Him, but you know Him because He abides with you and will be in you . . . In that day you will know that I am in My Father, and you in Me, and I in you . . . I in them and You in Me, that they may be perfected in unity, so that the world may know that You sent Me, and loved them, even as You have loved Me.*

7. *1 Corinthians 13:4 Love is patient, love is kind and is not jealous; love does not brag and is not arrogant.*

Love is not a feeling, a concept, an idea, or a philosophy. Love is a person. Love is Jesus Christ. So if you are confused about who Jesus is, read 1 Corinthians 13 and replace the word *love* with *Yeshua*. Because you are in Him, this passage becomes a beautiful description of who you truly are.

8. *1 Corinthians 13:4-8 Love is patient, love is kind and is not jealous; love does not brag and is not arrogant, does not act unbecomingly; it does not seek its own, is not provoked, does not take into account a wrong suffered, does not rejoice in unrighteousness, but rejoices with the truth; bears all things, believes all things, hopes all things, endures all things. Love never fails.*

In 2 Corinthians 5:18, Paul describes the boundless goodness of the reconciliation of Jesus to mankind. God doesn't count our trespasses against us. Isn't this the same love as defined in 1 Corinthians 13? In reconciling us to Him, Jesus doesn't seek His own, Jesus is not provoked, He does not take into account a wrong suffered, He does not rejoice in unrighteousness, He rejoices in the truth. Jesus bears all things, believes all things, hopes all things, and He endures all things. Jesus never fails because Jesus is God and God is love, and love does not fail.

SIXTEEN

BEING LOVE IN THE DARKNESS

You are the daughter, the son, of the Father...and until you truly see who you are, you will always struggle in vain to be who you think you should be and do what you think you should do. And when you do see who you are, you will also see others in that same light.

LOVE IS THE CURRENCY OF GOD

We have seen that just as Jesus was in this world, now you are the light created to shine in the darkness. Love is the most staggering power in the universe. We see that all things consist in Jesus, created by and for Him, and in Him all things are held together. So then, it is literally love that holds the universe together. Since there is no fear in love, there is no need for fear in you.

We have often heard the phrase about being light in the darkness. But without love, there is no light. It's easy to do good works when it feeds our ego. People may do the right thing for love or because it brings them a sense of joy or significance. But as we have seen, without love, all of our efforts are nothing. So to be light, our works must be rooted in love and not the ego.

So trying to love more might seem like the way to be light. But it actually begins with letting go. Let go of the need to be seen and heard and then, do and speak. Let go of the need to be noticed and then you are free to love without your ego being snared by pride. Let go of finding your identity in others and then you can see them as your Father sees them. Let go of the need to protect yourself and you can love without condition.

Here is a good motto to live by: Surrender all condemnation of others. It doesn't serve you.

Sure, you can condemn others if you like, but when you do, you are only holding a sword over your own head and so suffer yourself. Remember that to love the least is to love Jesus Himself. He takes the way we treat others personally, especially the weak and outcast. According to Jesus, we are to love family, friends, sinners, and enemies, all as if they were us.

In Jesus' time, prostitutes were the scourge of the earth and His teaching to the religious leaders was, "let him without sin cast the first stone." What is your attitude toward those who you consider to be the deviant members of society today?

Better to leave condemnation to others.

That includes condemnation of yourself. When the Father's love for you is made real, you will love yourself, your enemies, your friends, and above all, Him in a way you had never thought possible.

REFLECT ON THESE QUESTIONS

1. Make a short list of people who you think are sinners. What you do to them is what you do to Jesus, He said. Now imagine loving them as if they *were* Jesus. How does doing so make you feel?

_____

_____

2. Many Christians think of themselves as failures and can't receive love from the Father. Do you have trouble accepting or embracing the Father's incredible love for you who feel, like most of us, the least among all, because of your failures? Why?

_____

_____

3. In what tangible way can you demonstrate the extravagant love of your Father to a person who you think of as a sinner? Christ is in you and you in Him, so rather than telling them *about* Jesus, how could you *be* Jesus to them?

_____

_____

SCRIPTURES AND REFLECTIONS FROM THE MEDITATION

1. ***Matthew 6:34*** *So do not worry about tomorrow; for tomorrow will care for itself. Each day has enough trouble of its own.* ***1 Peter 5:6-7*** *Therefore humble yourselves under the mighty hand of God, that He may exalt you at the proper time, casting all your anxiety on Him, because He cares for you.*

To worry is to meditate on the power of a negative circumstance. We have no ability to "let go" by ourselves. Only when we see that we are held, loved, and cared for by our Father can we rest in the peace of Yeshua. Humility is not humiliation. In surrendering to the embrace of the Father, you will find that He lifts you up. Rather than being humiliated, you are exalted. Every fear, worry, and anxiety is burned away in the consuming fire of His love. Your Father tells you not to worry because releasing anxiety is both possible and beneficial. Worry is only faith in the storm. Rest is the reward of trust.

2. ***Ephesians 3:17-19*** *That you, being rooted and grounded in love, may be able to comprehend with all the saints what is the breadth and length and height and depth, and to know the love of Christ which surpasses knowledge, that you may be filled up to all the fullness of God.*

Your Father is perfect. He's better than you think, and you can't imagine Him to be better than He is. When you surrender to His embrace, you can fully rest in the knowledge that He will love you into complete wholeness, no matter how broken you think you have become.

3. ***Matthew 25:40*** *Truly I say to you, to the extent that you did it to one of these brothers of Mine, even the least of them, you did it to Me.*

2 Corinthians 5:14-16 *For the love of Christ controls us, having concluded this, that one died for all, therefore all died; and He died for all, so that they who live might no longer live for themselves, but for Him who died and rose again on their behalf. Therefore from now on we recognize no one according to the flesh.*

Galatians 3:28 *There is neither Jew nor Greek, there is neither slave nor free man, there is neither male nor female; for you are all one in Christ Jesus.*

4. *1 Timothy 1:16* NIV *But for that very reason I was shown mercy so that in me, the worst of sinners, Christ Jesus might display his immense patience as an example for those who would believe in Him and receive eternal life.*

5. *John 17:22* *The glory which You have given Me I have given to them, that they may be one, just as We are one.*

6. *Mark 12:30, 31* *"Love the Lord your God with all your heart, and with all your soul, and with all your mind, and with all your strength."* . . . *."You shall love your neighbor as yourself." There is no other commandment greater than these.*

God is complete, never divided. Yet He lives in you fully and completely. Though in this world of form we appear to be in different costumes, Christ is never divided. Therefore we are indeed one in spirit. That spirit realm is eternal, and this physical dimension is temporal. See yourself as one with the person you are blessing, giving to, loving, and you will see that the grace you release comes into you. This is why judging is so deadly. For we are one, even with those we hate.

7. *1 Corinthians 12:27* ESV *Now you are the body of Christ and individually members of it.* *Romans 12:5* *We, who are many, are one body in Christ, and individually members one of another.*

SEVENTEEN

LET ALL YOUR TROUBLES FALL AWAY

If you are complete, nothing can truly threaten you.

THE ART OF FORGIVENESS

What does it mean to let all your troubles fall away? Can it really be that simple? Yes. Simple but not always easy.

Although pain is universal, suffering from that pain comes from grievance which stands like a plank in your eye, blocking your sight of the light and keeping you in darkness. As you let go of these grievances you will see the light that is already there.

The term we use for letting go is forgiveness. To For-Give. And the best way to forgive is to let go before it becomes a problem. And by letting go, we are talking of letting go of the grievance itself, meaning to not record the record of that wrong in our minds to start with.

Even while being terribly abused, Jesus was able to forgive those beating Him. *Forgive them, for they know not what they do,* He said. In doing so, Jesus was showing us the way of radical forgiveness—the kind that doesn't record the wrong done to us even if it is being done. This is true love because love holds no record of wrong, as Paul wrote.

This kind of love, expressed in forgiveness, is the core evidence of the Spirit within us as the sons and daughters of God. Without it, our power is stripped. With it, we soar like eagles in a world bound by condemnation.

Notice who is the greatest recipient of this kind of forgiveness. You. When you let go of offense, you let a huge weight fall from you and you feel free.

Our natural understanding of forgiveness is to absolve someone from their sin, but the Way of Jesus shows us true forgiveness which attributes innocence to the one attacking us. Forgive them, why? Forgive them *because they don't know what they are doing and so are innocent.* They are bound in the same insanity that grips the whole world.

Take the plank out of your own eye and you will see to help others through love. Take the plank of offense that blinds you from your own beauty and you will see that you are the light of the world and your whole bodily experience will be full of light.

As we let go of the offense we have toward others for their trespasses, we find forgiveness ourselves, just as Jesus prayed in the Lord's prayer. If we don't, we stand condemned in this life. Forgive our trespasses *as* we forgive those who trespass against us. To be angry with someone who has wronged you may seem unavoidable, but according to Jesus you only join them in their darkness.

Instead, forgive. Forgive 70 times 7, which simply means constantly, always, forever. Forgiveness is perhaps your greatest power in this life because it is the means of surrender that most radically shows you light and freedom in any situation.

REFLECT ON THESE QUESTIONS

1. In the story of the husband and wife, which character did you more identify with and why?

_____

_____

2. If you believed you could set yourself free or bring a greater revelation of freedom by forgiving an enemy, what would you say to that person to let them know they were no longer bound by your judgment?

_____

_____

3. Imagine for a moment what your relationships would be like if you practiced active forgiveness and recorded no wrong in your mind. Would you find yourself at peace from the storms in life? Could you, like Jesus, sleep in the boat while the storm rages?

_____

_____

ACTIVATION

Write down three things in your life situation that persistently annoy you. Things like the way people drive, or certain kinds of music, or the politics of certain leaders. If you are in a group, share them aloud.

Now take an emotional journey and imagine letting go of your condemnation of those things. How does doing so make you feel? Frustration? Feelings of unfairness? Or peace and freedom? There is no right way of feeling—no condemnation of you. Just notice how you feel and be honest. If you are in a group, discuss your feelings.

_____

_____

SCRIPTURES AND REFLECTIONS

1. *Luke 6:42* *How can you say to your brother, 'Brother, let me take out the speck that is in your eye,' when you yourself do not see the log that is in your own eye? You hypocrite, first take the log out of your own eye, and then you will see clearly to take out the speck that is in your brother's eye.*

2. *Luke 23:34 But Jesus was saying, "Father, forgive them; for they do not know what they are doing." And they cast lots, dividing up His garments among themselves.*

3. *Colossians 3:12-14 So, as those who have been chosen of God, holy and beloved, put on a heart of compassion, kindness, humility, gentleness and patience; bearing with one another, and forgiving each other, whoever has a complaint against anyone; just **as the Lord forgave you**, so also should you. Beyond all these things put on love, which is the perfect bond of unity.*

To love is to forgive. If we could forgive our enemies without loving them, Jesus would have never given the command to love our enemies. To forgive someone isn't to say that what they did was okay. It's to extend mercy in spite of what was done. This is bearing with one another, just as Christ has done for us. True forgiveness is to set someone free from your judgments and punishments.

4. *Matthew 18:18 Truly I say to you, whatever you bind on earth shall have been bound in heaven; and whatever you loose on earth shall have been loosed in heaven.*

Look closely here at the wording. "Shall have been" indicates that what happens here in time reflects what already is in eternity. The standard of heaven is not lowered by our blindness, sin, failure, and darkness here on earth. Rather, we are to shine with the radiant love of a superior kingdom. So we are not on a mission to bring earth to heaven, but heaven to earth. The way we do that is to recognize what already exists in heaven and reflect it here on earth.

5. *1 Thessalonians 5:4-5 But you, brethren, are not in darkness, that the day would overtake you like a thief; for you are all sons of light and sons of day. We are not of night nor of darkness.*

6. *Matthew 5:21-22 You have heard that the ancients were told, 'You shall not commit murder' and 'Whoever commits murder will be liable to the court.' But I say to you that everyone who is angry with his brother* (or sister) *will be guilty . . . And whoever says, 'You Fool!' shall be guilty . . .*

Just as Jesus taught that lust was essentially the same as adultery, here He makes the case plain that what people think is ultimately as ruinous as what they do, because both thought and action separate them from their true identity. To be angry with someone who has wronged you may seem unavoidable, but according to Jesus you only join them in their darkness.

EIGHTEEN
GIVING IS RECEIVING

When you give peace to an enemy,
you are receiving that same peace.

HOW THE LAST BECOMES FIRST

We have seen that just as Jesus was in this world, now you are the light created to shine in the darkness. Love is the most staggering power in the universe. We see that all things consist in Jesus, created by and for Him, and in Him all things are held together. So then it is literally love that holds the universe together. Since there is no fear in love there is no fear in you. This is how you bring peace in the midst of strife and conflict.

We are built with the *desire* to receive but the *need* to give. It's a *need* because without giving, we can't actually receive. Giving *is* receiving, however opposite the way of the world this seems. Most importantly we give our surrender, our faith, our identity over to who we are in Christ.

In this way it is as Jesus taught, that giving is more blessed than receiving. How letting go actually imparts to you is illogical until you realize that when you give to another, you're giving to yourself. Try it and you will see. Don't give so that you can receive, just give without expecting any return or praise, and see how it affects you.

Jesus went as far as saying that when we loan, we should do so without expecting any repayment of that loan. How opposite this is to the way of the world which is bound in law—an eye for an eye. A dollar for a dollar. Even if we wrestle with this teaching, as we all do, it elevates giving to a status not unlike forgiving.

Forgiving and giving are two sides of the same coin and both define love at its core. Both are forms of letting go.

Have you felt it your due diligence to only give when you know your gift will be used correctly? You question because it seems illogical to be wasteful, or to enable an addiction, especially when the gift could be better used. The disciples felt this same way when a year's wages were poured out on Jesus feet in an act of worship.

But our giving reinforces our identity as much as it ministers to the need before us. When you give to a homeless person on the street, regardless of what they do with your gift, your giving in and of itself blesses you. So then, give to others. Give grace. Give love. Give of your material possessions.

In so doing, you give grace and love to yourself. Though seemingly depleted (last) you discover a life of abundance (first). This is how the last becomes first.

REFLECT ON THESE QUESTIONS

1. When was the last time you gave someone something, not because of who they were or what you might expect in return, but only for the sake of giving?

_____

_____

2. If Jesus asks us to give without expecting anything in return, does He give without any condition as well? Or does He require your allegiance in return for His gift to you?

_____

_____

3. Explain how forgiveness and giving selflessly are two sides of the same coin.

_____

_____

ACTIVATION

If you are in a group, give a word of kindness to everyone in the group before you leave. See how it lifts your spirit to its natural state in Christ. Today or tomorrow, make a point of giving something to a stranger for no reason other than to give. Notice how it makes you feel. Now do it every day. Whether it's a word of kindness to a clerk or a five dollar bill to a homeless person, do it because it is what you do as the son or daughter of the Father. It's who you are under the costume you wear to project another identity.

SCRIPTURES AND REFLECTIONS FROM THE MEDITATION

1. ***Galatians 6:8*** *For the one who sows to his own flesh will from the flesh reap corruption, but the one who sows to the Spirit will from the Spirit reap eternal life.*

2. ***Luke 6:35*** *But love your enemies, and do good, and lend, expecting nothing in return; and your reward will be great, and you will be sons of the Most High; for He Himself is kind to ungrateful and evil men.*

3. ***Romans 6:22-23*** *But now having been freed from sin and enslaved to God, you derive your benefit, resulting in sanctification, and the outcome, eternal life. For the wages of sin is death, but the free gift of God is eternal life in Christ Jesus our Lord.*

Being enslaved to God may sound negative, but remember that the Son has set you "free indeed" and in that freedom, find a beautiful liberty, sanctification, and eternal life in your union with God in Christ.

4. ***Romans 5:20*** *The Law came in so that the transgression would increase; but where sin increased, grace abounded all the more.*

5. ***Matthew 25:40*** *Truly I say to you, to the extent that you did it to one of these brothers of Mine, even the least of them, you did it to Me.*

6. ***Luke 9:24*** *For whoever wishes to save his life will lose it, but whoever loses his life for My sake, he is the one who will save it.*

7. *Luke 6:37-38* *Do not judge, and you will not be judged; and do not condemn, and you will not be condemned; pardon, and you will be pardoned. Give, and it will be given to you. They will pour into your lap a good measure—pressed down, shaken together, and running over. For by your standard of measure it will be measured to you in return.*

This verse is often used to uphold the principle of giving in terms of money, but if you read the verse in context, you can clearly see that the context is not money, but the giving of non-judgment, which is grace.

8. *Luke 10:36-37* *"Which of these three do you think proved to be a neighbor to the man who fell into the robbers' hands?" And He said, "The one who showed mercy toward him." Then Jesus said to him, "Go and do the same."*

Our compassion unifies us. In this story, Jesus uses the outcast to illustrate a love that is for all mankind. Our position, reputation, heritage, religion, or nationality have no power to justify a lack of compassion for another person made in the image and likeness of God.

NINETEEN

ENEMIES AND FRIENDS

Whether from within or outside,
your only true enemy is fear.

REVEALING RELATIONSHIPS

Whenever we speak of union, of seeing as Jesus, we find that included in that, are not just the people we love. The people we are called to love are always a much larger group than the people we know. Yet within the circle of people we know, there is still the judgment of preference. We like some more than we like others. Beyond even the people we like, there are those that we find difficult to like. You might even say that loving them is impossible.

We have placed faith in another person's ability to hurt us, and so we make them our enemy. In the same way, when you see your own ability to bring pain into your own life, you might find that you have become an enemy in your own eyes. Release them from your judgments and punishments. Let them go, and in so doing, you forgive yourself.

Just as difficult as an enemy, is a friend, because in them you often place your significance, your identity, your trust, your faith, your hope. You unwittingly become dependent on their loyalty and the joy they bring to you. So then, you demand something without even realizing it, and you fear the loss of that loyalty and joy.

Is this not a form of addictive clinging more than a true love that expects nothing in return? Most people use their relationships more like drugs than as the expression of authentic love.

True love is measured by how you love when you are not loved, how you honor when you are dishonored. Can you give love with no expectation of return? Or is your love primarily fueled by the love shown to you? Is it dependent upon the love of another?

Surrender the fear you have of your enemies and the expectations you have of your friends. Hold them of no account because this is what Jesus tells us when He says to 'hate' (hold of no account) those closest to us.

Release your enemies from your judgments and release your friends from your expectations. Neither serve you. Rather live secure that you are eternally loved by a good Father who has given Himself to be one with you without condition.

In our lives, we may choose to leave a relationship in which we are subject to abuse, and that's fine. But even then, the condemnation you harbor in your heart will follow you like a dark cloud. Let it go. You don't have to stay with the one who is abusing you, but neither does your grievance have to say with you. Only you can let that go.

REFLECT ON THESE QUESTIONS

1. Have you ever been the recipient of a love that expects absolutely nothing in return? From whom and how did you experience this love?

_____

_____

2. Have you ever given true love to someone close without any expectation of return? Write down their name. Can you continue to love them in this way?

_____

_____

3. Imagine someone you are or have been romantically involved with. What kind of suffering do you experience when they disappoint your expectations of them? How could you be free from that suffering without them changing?

_____

_____

4. Do you live up to all the expectations you place on yourself? If you only love those who meet your expectations of them, how can you love yourself?

_____

_____

SCRIPTURES AND REFLECTIONS

1. ***Mark 4:39-40*** *He got up and rebuked the wind and said to the sea, "Hush, be still." And the wind died down and it became perfectly calm. And He said to them, "Why are you afraid? Do you still have no faith?"*

2. **Luke 6:35** *But love your enemies, and do good, and lend, expecting nothing in return; and your reward will be great, and you will be sons of the Most High.*

Take a moment to meditate on this perspective of your Father. There is none higher. Nothing is above your Father in greatness, in glory, in power, in strength, in all of time and eternity. And He has raised you, His son, His daughter, up with Him. This is resurrected life.

Matthew 5:46 *For if you love those who love you, what reward do you have?*

3. ***Matthew 5:39*** *Do not resist an evil person, but whoever slaps you on the right cheek, turn the other to him also.*

Grace and mercy do not say that evil behavior is okay. It is saying that there is no storm, no wave, that can rise above the love of Christ alive within you. The kindness of God is the very light that leads the blind toward sight.

4. 1 Corinthians 13:5 (Love) *does not dishonor others, it is not self-seeking, it is not easily angered, it keeps no record of wrongs.*

5. Luke 14:26 *If anyone comes to Me, and does not hate his own father and mother and wife and children and brothers and sisters, yes, and even his own life, he cannot be My disciple.*

Let no other person be empowered to define your identity. Do not even try to define it yourself. That alone is reserved for your Father. It is from that identity of love Himself that you can reflect His divine nature to be a father, husband, wife, brother, or sister in this life. Only in this way can you love as He loves.

TWENTY

FINDING SUPERMAN

*Let go of all that you thought you were, to discover who
you truly are, and so walk this earth as the son, the
daughter, of God in peace and power.*

BELIEVE IN THE NAME OF JESUS

We have read and heard much in churches and Bible studies about believing in the name of Jesus. But have you understood what that means? We've made a habit of ending prayers of thanksgiving by saying, "…in Jesus' name." We've made a habit of beginning prayers of petition by saying, "In Jesus' name…" There's no problem in this, but the term has become, for many in religious circles, a cultural norm without understanding of its original meaning.

In Western culture we use names as labels.

A name in the culture of Jesus represented a person's full identity and was followed by the name of their father. In the case of Jesus, it was Jesus the Messiah (Christ). A name represented one's identity, knitting them into the family line and affecting the way they acted, the way they were seen, and the authority that they carried.

The name or identity of Jesus is what you are in, because it's also in you, as Jesus said—"I in you and you in Me." He has brought you into the union of His divine nature. This is why Paul writes in describing our renewal in Jesus: *…a renewal in which there is no distinction between Greek and Jew, circumcised and uncircumcised, barbarian, Scythian, slave and freeman,* **but Christ is all, and in all.** (Col. 3:11)

Whenever you do anything "in the name" of Jesus, you are doing and being in the identity of Jesus. To believe in His name is to trust in the inclusion of yourself into that identity and so become a partaker of the Divine nature.

In this way, you, like the first Adam and Eve before the fall, are the son, the daughter, of God, because you have been grafted into the second Adam, Jesus, who is the Son of God.

From this faith of His identity and your own in Him, nothing is impossible. In His identity you are filled with His glory, empowered by His Spirit because He gave you the glory that the Father gave Him, as He made clear. You aren't standing on earth making a petition to a God who is far off in an untouchable celestial fortress. You are right now, seated in heavenly places, and now your prayers are conversations and your requests are decrees to be established on earth as it is in heaven.

Letting go of your attachment to this world and anchoring your identity in heaven is the result of the renewed mind. And yet we forget daily, reverting back to an identity long dead. Thus, most of us live in sin (separation or missing the mark) most of the time, because whatever is not done in faith is sin (Rom. 14:23). In that old identity the world begins to master us, when in reality we have been empowered to overcome it in Christ.

But that doesn't change who you are as the son, the daughter, of the Father or you would be gaining and losing your sonship all the time, whenever you do or think anything that is not from faith. Sin doesn't change who you are, but it does radically affect your ability to be who you are and love as He loves, and it always leads to misery.

Let your heart be filled with gratitude because you are the son, the daughter of the Father. Now go and sin no more. And, thus, be who you are. Any other way of being will always darken your perception of the world, yourself, and your Father.

REFLECT ON THESE QUESTIONS

1. How often do you live from or in sin, rather than from or in faith as the son or daughter of the Father?

_____

_____

2. Jesus told us to abide in the vine, and that vine was Him. How would life be if you lived with the abiding awareness of your identity in Jesus?

_____

_____

3. Do you condemn yourself when you doubt or struggle to live in faith? Would knowing that the Father does not condemn you for this, but continues to draw you into knowing Him, cause you to be awed by His love for you?

_____

_____

SCRIPTURES AND REFLECTIONS FROM THE MEDITATION

1. *John 14:12-13 Truly, truly, I say to you, he who believes in Me, the works that I do, he will do also; and greater works than these he will do; because I go to the Father. Whatever you ask in My name, that will I do, so that the Father may be glorified in the Son.*

Have you ever seen a believer do greater works than Jesus? Think of the works Jesus did. And now He says you will do greater? And in doing greater, you will be expressing the glory of the Son on earth as it is in heaven. As His son, His daughter, this is your inheritance in this life.

2. *John 15:8, 16-17 ESV By this my Father is glorified, that you bear much fruit and so prove to be my disciples . . . I chose you and appointed you that you should go and bear fruit and that your fruit should abide, so that whatever you ask the Father in my name, He may give it to you. These things I command you, so that you will love one another.*

You can't bear fruit apart from union with Christ. It is the abiding presence of Christ's love within you that makes fruit naturally come forth.

3. *John 17:22-23 The glory which You have given Me I have given to them, that they may be one, just as We are one; I in them and You in Me, that they may be perfected in unity, so that the world may know that You sent Me, and loved them, even as You have loved Me.*

Our union with God and with each other is the key that opens the locked door that stands between the world and the love of the Father. Could it be that the world is blind because we have put on display division and judgment rather than unity and grace? Meditate on this phrase, "that the world may know."

4. *James 4:2-3 You do not have because you do not ask. You ask and do not receive, because you ask with wrong motives, so that you may spend it on your pleasures.*

By "spend on your pleasures," James means all that would satisfy the old mind, the flesh-body divorced from Christ. So much of what we ask for is motivated by our identification with our bodies and our relationships. Is it any wonder then that we ask amiss?

5. *Philippians 4:11-13 I have learned to be content in whatever circumstances I am. I know how to get along with humble means, and I also know how to live in prosperity; in any and every circumstance I have learned the secret of being filled and going hungry, both of having abundance and suffering need. I can do all things through Him who strengthens me.*

This passage is not just about enduring challenges, and it's not about placing mind over matter. Paul is revealing the power of the renewed mind to transform reality by seeing this world from divine perspective.

Luke 1:37 For nothing will be impossible with God. Mark 10:27 Looking at them, Jesus said, "With people it is impossible, but not with God; for all things are possible with God." Mark 9:23 And Jesus said to him, "'If You can? All things are possible to him who believes."

TWENTY-ONE
A NEW DECLARATION

Have This is your path: To work out your salvation with fear and trembling. With fear, because stepping off the shore of the old mind's certainty and engaging faith is offensive to that old mind and causes fear. With trembling because when you do so, you will soon find that the goodness of God makes you weak in the knees.

THE GREATEST OF THESE

To determine love to be the greatest among faith and hope is not to exercise preference, but rather priority. We know that there is no house that can stand without a foundation. So then, nothing you have learned can even exist if there is no foundation to build upon. The foundation of this Kingdom that you are both in and of is love.

You are becoming aware of the One in whose likeness you are reborn. You are no longer a child of the first Adam but a son of God by the grace of the last Adam. Now you live this resurrected life in His name, following that pathway of letting go in order to be who you truly are. In that place of surrender there is tremendous peace and power against the threat of the wind and waves of every storm that arises against you in this world. In that place of love, you master this world, instead of letting it master you.

Take time every day, every hour, every minute, to pause and let go. The journey of transformation is yours to take. You cannot borrow someone else's transformation. You can learn from the journey of another but each of us must take the journey for ourselves. Each journey may look vastly different. Don't judge one over another. Trust the Father to draw His children home. Let your heart and eyes open to the wonder of being a son and daughter of the Father. Taste now and see that He is so very good. Not of this world, you are now called to shine within it with a light that is also not of this world.

Let the Kingdom of God, the realm of heaven, Christ Himself, be released from within you to love the world around you. In this way His Kingdom comes, His will is done, on earth as it is in heaven.

ACTIVATION

Having come to the end of your journey through this study guide, take a minute and read the Five Declarations of *The Forgotten Way* aloud.

Our objective is not to create a new catechism but simply to help you understand your purpose here on earth from a fresh perspective. Read these five simple statements aloud and let each one mark your mind.

THE FORGOTTEN WAY

OUR DECLARATION

THE TRUTH

1) God, who is infinitely good and far more loving and kind to His children than any earthly mother or father imaginable, glorified His identity on earth by making mankind in His likeness, complete and in union with Him. But the first Adam embraced the knowledge of good and evil, so we were born into darkness, blinded to and separated from fellowship with our Father who does not condemn us.

2) We, as sons and daughters of the Father, are remade in the likeness of God. Yeshua, the second Adam, came as Light into all darkness and undid what the first Adam did, that we might experience the Father's life right now. This we call "eternal life." Even so, we put our identity in and so are mastered by one of two perceptions of reality each day. One is seen in flesh—the passing system of the world, darkened by the knowledge of good and evil, deceiving and enslaving us as we put our faith in it. The other realm is seen in the light through the power of the Holy Spirit—the eternal kingdom of the Father flowing with light and love without grievance.

THE WAY

3) Our journey now is to believe who we truly are, having been raised from the dark grave as new creatures into that realm of light with and in Yeshua. Belief in Yeshua is this: identifying with Him in His death, resurrection, and glory even now, He in us and we in Him. Our true identity is this: we are the sons and daughters of our Father, already made complete and whole; already at peace and full of power though we often forget, each day, whenever we are blinded to our true identity.

4) We will only see who we are, and thus be who we are, as we surrender our attachment to all other identities, which are like gods of a lesser power that block our vision of our true identity and so keep us in darkness. Our surrender is to deny our false selves, to take up the cross, to let go of all that holds us captive in this world, because we are in the world but not of it.

THE LIFE

5) To the extent we place our identity in His, we will be known for our extravagant love, which is the evidence of our true nature, risen with Christ. Walking in the realm of the Father's presence here on earth—abiding in the vine, who is Yeshua—we will find peace in the storms; we will walk on the troubled seas of our lives; we will not be poisoned by the lies of snakes; we will move mountains that appear insurmountable; we will heal all manner of sickness that twists minds and bodies.
The fruit of the Spirit will flow from us as living waters, because the manifestation of the kingdom of heaven on earth is love. And when we love, all will know: there goes one who walks in the Spirit and flies on the wings of an eagle.

REFLECT ON THESE QUESTIONS

Jesus said that all Scripture can be reduced to this one statement

1. How has your journey through *The Forgotten Way* changed your relationship with your God—Father, Son and Holy Spirit?

_____

_____

2. How has *The Forgotten Way* changed the way you see yourself as the son or daughter of the Father?

_____

_____

3. How has *The Forgotten Way* changed the way you see others?

_____

_____

SCRIPTURES AND REFLECTIONS FROM THE MEDITATION

1. *Galatians 3:27* *For all of you who were baptized into Christ have clothed yourselves with Christ.*
    2. *Luke 14:18-20* *But they all alike began to make excuses. The first said to him, 'I have bought a field and I must go out and see it. Please have me excused.' And another said, 'I have bought five yoke of oxen and I go to examine them. Please have me excused.' And another said, 'I have married a wife and therefore I cannot come.'*

3. *Matthew 25:1-9 Then the kingdom of heaven will be comparable to ten virgins, who took their lamps and went out to meet the bridegroom. Five of them were foolish, and five were prudent. For when the foolish took their lamps, they took no oil with them, but the prudent took oil in flasks along with their lamps. Now while the bridegroom was delaying, they all got drowsy and began to sleep. But at midnight there was a shout, "Behold, the bridegroom! Come out to meet him." Then all those virgins rose and trimmed their lamps. The foolish said to the prudent, "Give us some of your oil, for our lamps are going out." But the prudent answered, "No, there will not be enough for us and you too; go instead to the dealers and buy some for yourselves."*

4. **Matthew 16:24** *Jesus said to His disciples, "If anyone wishes to come after Me, he must deny himself, and take up his cross and follow Me."*

5. **John 17:16** *They are not of the world even as I am not of the world.*

6. **Mark 9:43** NIV *If your hand causes you to stumble, cut it off. It is better to enter life maimed than with two hands to go into hell (Gehenna) where the fire never goes out.*

7. *1 Corinthians 2:16 "Who has known the mind of the Lord, that he will instruct him?" But we have the mind of Christ.*

8. *Galatians 3:28 There is neither Jew nor Greek, there is neither slave nor free man, there is neither male nor female; for you are all one in Christ Jesus.* **Colossians 3:9-11** *Do not lie to one another, since you laid aside the old self with its evil practices, and have put on the new self who is being renewed to a true knowledge according to the image of the One who created him—a renewal in which there is no distinction between Greek and Jew, circumcised and uncircumcised, barbarian, Scythian, slave and freeman, but Christ is all, and in all.*

In Paul's letter to the Colossians, he even becomes more radical with this thought. He includes here the Scythians who were violent, hostile and rejected by the society and culture of the day. Think of the most hated, rejected, and outcast subcultures in our world today, and insert that group in place of "barbarian." Now understand how stunning this statement is. And yet you are none of these labels. You are in Christ and He is in you.

9. ***Ephesians 2:4-8*** *But God, being rich in mercy, because of His great love with which He loved us, even when we were dead in our transgressions, made us alive together with Christ (by grace you have been saved), and raised us up with Him, and seated us with Him in the heavenly places in Christ Jesus, so that in the ages to come He might show the surpassing riches of His grace in kindness toward us in Christ Jesus. For by grace you have been saved through faith; and that not of yourselves, it is the gift of God.* ***John 17:22-23*** *The glory which You have given Me I have given to them, that they may be one, just as We are one; I in them and You in Me, that they may be perfected in unity, so that the world may know that You sent Me, and loved them, even as You have loved Me.*

10. ***John 4:24*** *God is spirit and those who worship him must worship Him in spirit and truth.*

NOTES

NOTES

_____

_____

_____

_____

_____

_____

_____

_____

_____

_____

_____

_____

_____

_____

_____

_____

_____

NOTES